Creating Balance in Children:

Activities to Optimize Learning and Behavior

A Guide for Teachers and Parents
of Children Ages 5 to 14

Lorraine O. Moore, Ph.D.
and
Peggy Henrikson

Peytral Publications, Inc.
Minnetonka, MN

6143 4901   7/06

Publisher's Cataloging-in-Publication
(Provided by Quality Books, Inc.)

Moore, Lorraine O.
    Creating balance in children : activities to optimize
Learning and behavior : a guide for teachers and parents
of children ages 5 to 14 / Lorraine O. Moore, Peggy
Henrikson. -- 1st ed.

    p. cm.
    LCCN 2005921833
    ISBN 1890455385

    1. Child psychology. 2. Child development.
3. Educational psychology. 4. Activity programs in
education.   I. Henrikson, Peggy.   II. Title

    BF721.M66 2005   155.4
    QBI05-218

Peytral Publications, Inc.
PO Box 1162
Minnetonka, MN   55345-0162
Tel: 952-949-8707
Fax: 952-906-9777
Web: www.peytral.com

Table of Contents

*   indicates the activity can be completed in 5-10 minutes
** indicates the activity can be adapted to 5-10 minutes

* indicates the activity can be completed in 5-10 minutes
**indicates the activity can be adapted to be completed in 5-10 minutes

* indicates the activity can be completed in 5-10 minutes
**indicates the activity can be adapted to be completed in 5-10 minutes

Dedication

The authors lovingly dedicate this book to Ben, Emma, Erin, and Paige and all the children of the world. We also dedicate it to all adults who give generously of their time and skills to help children grow into happy, healthy adults.

The Purpose of This Book

If you have been attracted to this book, we applaud you, because you are interested in actively supporting children, our world's most precious resources. This fast-paced, changing world has many pressures and pulls, both towards high performance and achievement and towards a wide range of unhealthy influences, from junk food and too much television to drugs, alcohol, and violence. Physical, mental, and emotional imbalances, even if not extreme, can have detrimental effects on children's learning, behavior, health, and relationships, and can cause a malaise of the spirit. Research has shown that depression, loneliness, anger, aggression, nervousness, and worry are on the rise in children as a whole. Attention deficit and hyperactivity are being diagnosed with alarming freqency, and the increase in childhood obesity has become a national concern.

The purpose of this book is twofold: to help rebalance children when imbalance occurs and also to help prevent it from occurring. The book provides fun and thought-provoking activities and resources for the many concerned teachers, parents, and childcare providers who wish to help bring more balance into children's lives. It also presents options for children that will help them prevent imbalance and maintain health and stability in this unbalanced world. The activities introduce children to the meaning of balance and its importance. Most significantly, they help children actually create and/or maintain balance in the physical, cognitive, and emotional/social aspects of their lives and also nourish their spirits, thus encouraging a depth of strength, courage, and caring.

The activities involve writing, drawing and other artwork, discussing and brainstorming, creative movement, music, and games. The easy-to-follow format delineates the purpose of each activity, its approximate timeframe, the materials needed, and step-by-step instructions. The activities offer considerable flexibility, ranging in length from five minutes to one hour, and some include parts that can be given at different times or possible extensions. You may need to adjust the activities to make them age-appropriate for your children, and in many cases, suggestions are provided for how this might be accomplished. Use your creativity and your own ideas along with those presented, and have fun!

This book includes three main sections of activities, plus an Appendix and a Resources section. Following are descriptions of each.

Section 1, The Meaning of Balance
We are constantly adjusting one aspect or another of our lives to maintain an overall balance. Certainly we all have our ups and downs, but when children are in overall balance, they can recover quickly from physical and emotional stresses. On the whole, they are able to think and reason clearly. They have a sense of meaning in their lives, they feel they belong, and they sense that life has purpose. The activities in this section draw out what children already know or intuit about balance and also fill in the gaps in their understanding so they appreciate the meaning and importance of balance to their learning, behavior, health, relationships, and general well-being. These activities encourage the children to think about the concept of balance in their lives and include a working model of balance and a self-assessment. Projects

from this section give the children a foundation of understanding for activities in the rest of the book and can be put into Balance Journals that the children make in Activity 3.

Section 2, Achieving Balance Through Meeting the Needs of the Body, Mind, and Heart

Although it would seem that this section could be divided into three (body, mind, and heart), it is presented as one because of the intrinsic interconnection between these three aspects of our being. Each affects the others so profoundly that anything that benefits one benefits the others, and anything that takes away from the functioning of one takes away from the functioning of the others and the outcome of them working together. Although you will find that some activities in this section focus on physical aspects and others on cognitive or emotional/social aspects, all are interwoven.

Thus, this section has activities built around such factors as nutrition, movement, sleep and rest, sensory stimuli, and environmental influences. It also emphasizes the importance of our emotions and provides activities that help children understand their emotions and achieve emotional balance in their lives. "Emotional intelligence" is becoming more and more recognized as vital to children's success in all aspects of their lives, including social relationships and learning. In addition, Section 2 presents activities that promote a balance between the right brain and left brain, enhancing both analytical thinking as well as creativity and encouraging better problem-solving and more cognitive exploration. Activities involving sensory stimulation boost cognitive development as well as physical development and thus also affect the emotional/social aspects of a child's life.

Section 3, Nourishing the Spirit

Meaning is the overall context that permeates everything in a person's life and can help provide motivation for taking care of the other three aspects of body, mind, and heart. If properly developed, this context can give a child a tremendous boost in life and sound inner direction. The activities in this section draw out the inner spirit of the child. They help children become aware of their connection with all things and their own place in the world. They promote caring, respect, joy, and other aspects of the inner spirit. Activities in this section also stimulate a sense of wonder at the intelligence and purposeful nature of the universe.

Appendix

The Appendix includes further information for some activities and convenient, reproducible activity sheets for those activities that require them.

Resources

The Resources section adds another dimension of value with a list of helpful, related books for adults as well as a list for children. Readers are encouraged to delve more deeply into areas of special interest or concern.

In the face of research and obvious evidence, we can no longer question the necessity of helping children to become more balanced in body, mind, and heart. It is up to caring adults to provide not only models of balance in an unbalanced world but guidance to help bring more balance into children's lives and help them maintain it. Perhaps it can even be said that the future of the world is "in the balance."

Section 1

The Meaning of Balance

Activity 1

What Is Balance?

Purpose of this activity: This activity draws out what children already know or intuit about balance. It helps them to more fully understand the concept and generalize from just physical balance to balance in their lives.

Timeframe: about 45 minutes, depending on the length of discussion

What you need: Balance and Me Appendix Activity 1 and a pencil or pen for each child

What to do:

1. Start with a discussion of balance. Ask the following questions and pause for the children to answer: *"Who has been on a seesaw? ... Who has ridden a bicycle? ... Who has walked along a fallen log or along a tree branch? ... What do you need to do all these things? ... Yes, balance.*

   "What happens on a seesaw if one person is much bigger than the other? ... What would make you fall over when you're riding your bike or walking along a log? ... How does it help when walking a log to hold your arms out to your sides?"

   Lead the children into the understanding that too much weight on one side will pull you off balance and that your weight has to be evenly distributed to balance well, even if it is constantly being adjusted from one side to the other.

   Tell them they'll be thinking and talking more about balance, because it's important in many parts of their lives—not just on seesaws or riding their bikes.

2. Pass out the Appendix Activity 1, and make sure everyone has a pen or pencil. Ask them to complete the sentences on the sheet, and tell them to have fun with it. It is not a test—just something to get them thinking.

3. Ask for volunteers to share what they've written. Discuss their answers, leading the children to the conclusion that too much of one thing creates imbalance, which doesn't work very well in life, just as it doesn't work very well on a seesaw.

Notes

Activity 2

The Wheel of Balance

Purpose of this activity: We each have a body, mind, heart, and spirit. To have our lives go smoothly, we need to pay attention to and take care of all four of these aspects. This activity introduces children to a model of balance represented as a wheel made up of these four aspects of ourselves. If any aspects in our wheel of balance are not supported, our wheel won't roll very well! (See the Appendix for background information and the Wheel of Balance Model.)

Timeframe: 45 minutes to one hour. The writing part of the activity for older children can be a separate activity, if necessary.

What you need: one copy of the Appendix Activity 2 Wheel of Balance and coloring utensils for each child for drawing and another copy for each child who can write. You might want to use a chalkboard, whiteboard, or flipchart to record ideas.

What to do:

1. Give each child a copy of the Appendix Activity 2 Wheel of Balance and drawing utensils.

2. Tell the children the circle represents each person's life. It is divided into four parts, because we each have a body, mind, heart, and spirit. As you discuss each of these aspects of our lives, have the children label each quadrant. In order to have room for drawings, ask them to label the quadrants between the inner and outer circles, using the circumference of the inner circle as a baseline. (For younger children, you can copy the form and hand label the quadrants, then make copies of the labeled form for the children.) As you discuss the four aspects, allow the children to come up with their own definitions and descriptions, but feel free to prompt them if they get stuck. A Wheel of Balance Model is also included in Appendix Activity 2 (for your use and the sake of discussion).

3. Ask the children to illustrate the four aspects of their lives by drawing pictures in each of the four quadrants to represent that aspect of their lives. For example, in the body quadrant, they might draw pictures of food and/or the physical activities they do. Although the other areas aren't tangible like the physical, challenge the children to use their creativity in representing them with drawings.

4. Give children who can write another Wheel of Balance form after they have completed their drawings. Ask them to list in each quadrant what they are doing to take care of and pay attention to each of the four aspects of their lives, then to draw a line and list some new things they can do in addition to what they are doing. (With younger children, talk with them about how they might pay attention to and support each aspect of their lives. List their ideas on a board or flipchart, and help them brainstorm new ones.)

5. When they have finished drawing and listing, ask them to take a look at their wheels and their lists. Are some of the parts more full of drawings than others? Are some of the lists more lengthy than others? Explain that to have our lives roll smoothly along, we need to pay attention to and take care of all four of these aspects. Ask what would happen to a wheel if part of it were missing or smaller than the others. (It wouldn't roll very well!) You might want to draw such a wheel on the board or a flipchart to make the point.

6.   Ask the children to think of new ways they can pay attention to and take care of the parts of their lives that need more attention, and list these below the first list.

7.   Ask them to choose one of the things they listed and start putting it into action in their lives.

8.   Tell the children that, over a period of time, you'll be sharing with them more ideas about how to help their wheels of life roll more smoothly.

"Just as your car runs more smoothly and requires less energy to go faster and farther when the wheels are in perfect alignment, you perform better when your thoughts, feelings, emotions, goals, and values are in balance."
—Brian Tracy

Notes

Activity 3

Creating Balance Journals

Purpose of this activity: Having the children create journals in which to keep their thoughts, ideas, stories, drawings, and other records of activities around a theme helps them to personalize and enhance the meaning of the theme. Journals also serve as ready resources and references and are accumulative accounts of the exploration process in which the children are engaged. In this activity, the children create the covers for Balance Journals in which to keep the writings and drawings about balance that they generate while doing the activities in the first section of this book, The Meaning of Balance. It is best to have already done Activity 1, What Is Balance?, and Activity 2, The Wheel of Balance, so the children are familiar with the concept of balance. Those activity sheets can be inserted into the covers of their journals.

Timeframe: up to 30 minutes to create the journal

What you need: for each child, two 8½-x-11-inch pages of heavy-weight colored paper, solid-color wallpaper, or other appropriate material; a three-hole punch; brass hole fasteners, yarn, or ribbon to hold the covers together; and drawing or painting supplies such as crayons, markers, or paint and brushes. Covers could be laminated, if you wish. Depending upon the age of the children, folders can also make suitable journal covers.

What to do:

1. Have the children create covers for their journals out of sturdy colored paper or any other kind of durable material on which they can write, draw, and/or paint. Punch, or have the children punch, both covers with three holes for binding.

2. Ask them to write Balance Journal and their names on the front. If you wish, you may also have them make a symbol or draw a representation of the concept of balance on the front cover. At a later time, they may want to use the back cover for writing words or drawing pictures of what they do to help themselves stay in balance.

3. Have the children attach the covers with fasteners, yarn, ribbon, or whatever works best for you, allowing for pages to be inserted.

4. Have the children hole-punch their activity sheets from the first two activities, What Is Balance? and The Wheel of Balance, and insert them into their journals. As they complete the rest of the activities in the first section of this book, those can be added.

5. Collect the journals from the children, and keep them in a central place so they are accessible for future use.

Notes

Activity 4

Learning About Balance Through Self-Care

Purpose of this activity: Learning about ways to be in balance is a life-long process. Self-care is the cornerstone for addressing what our bodies, minds, hearts, and spirits need to obtain a state of balance and to rebalance as needed. The purpose of this activity is to introduce children to the idea of self-care and how self-care can help balance their bodies, minds, hearts, and spirits.

Timeframe: 15-45 minutes, depending upon how many of the four parts you choose to do in one timeframe

What you need: for each child, one copy each of the four Learning about Balance through Self-Care activity sheets (Appendix Activities 3, 4, 5, and 6)

What to do:

1. Introduce this activity by telling the children that they will be learning ways to help themselves balance their bodies, minds, hearts, and spirits through self-care (things they can do to take care of themselves). You may need to take a few moments to talk about what self-care means, emphasizing that when we are younger we are more dependent upon others for our care, but as we gain in age and experience, we are more able to be responsible for ourselves.

2. Distribute copies of the four activity sheets that cover the four areas of self-care involved in this activity (or as many sheets/areas as you wish to cover at this time). If you are choosing to do one area of care at a time, you may want to pass out the first sheet only: Self-Care of My Body. You may want to share the material orally with younger children who are unable to read the text and have them orally respond to the ideas in each area.

3. For each care area, first cover the information about that area, and then share the examples listed for each area. Note that these examples are generated from the letters in the word BALANCE.

4. After going over the examples for a specific area (such as the body), ask the children to add other ways in which they can take care of their bodies, minds, or whatever area you are addressing.

Note: Have the children put these pages in their Balance Journals to refer to (if they made them), and add ways of self-care for each area as they learn about them.

<u>Notes</u>

Activity 5

Stoplight Self-Assessment

Purpose of this activity: Often we don't stop to evaluate how we are feeling, so signs of imbalance can go unnoticed and cause negative repercussions in our lives. This activity helps children to check in with themselves and notice when something is out of balance. It encourages them to find solutions to any imbalance in their bodies, minds, or emotions so their learning and behavior don't suffer as a result but are supported in a positive way.

Timeframe: 45 minutes to one hour

What you need: green, yellow, and red 3-inch circles of paper (deciding how many you'll need after you read the activity); writing utensils; a flipchart, poster board, whiteboard, or chalkboard

What to do:

1. On a table, set out three piles of green, yellow, and red paper circles, respectively. Tell the children that they are going to play Stoplight.

2. Introduce this activity by asking the children to stop and reflect on how they are feeling in this moment.

   First ask them to silently consider how the different parts of their bodies feel, inside and out. Are their bodies feeling great, so-so, or not so good? (You may want to adjust these words to fit your group.) Give the children time to check in. If their bodies are feeling great, i.e., healthy, comfortable, and strong, have them come up and get a green circle. If their bodies are feeling so-so, meaning not great but not awful either, have them pick up a yellow circle, and if they are feeling not so good or really bad, a red circle.

   Then ask them how peaceful their minds are. If their minds are very peaceful, have them come up and get a green circle. If their minds are just a little busy and not quite ready to settle down, have them get a yellow circle. If their minds are jumping around like monkeys from tree to tree and not at all ready to settle down, have them pick up a red circle.

   Now ask the children to consider their emotions in the moment. Do they feel happy? Pick up a green circle. A bit upset or not really happy? A yellow circle. Sad, angry, or otherwise yucky? A red circle.

3. Tell the children to take stock of their stoplight colors. Tell them that:

   GREEN means being in a state of balance and ready to learn and take part in activities. Green means GO.

   YELLOW means being in a state of caution. Those with yellow circles need to pay attention to what is going on in their bodies, their thinking, or their feelings. It means LOOK OUT.

   RED means being in a state of imbalance. Those with red circles need to STOP and figure out what is out of balance in their bodies, their thinking, or their feelings. Then they need to do what they can to correct the imbalance(s).

4. Ask the children to share their thoughts about what makes them feel good and what seems to get in the way of learning and participating in activities either on their own or with others. Record their answers on a flipchart, poster board, whiteboard, or chalkboard. From the ideas the children generate, create the following general categories, listing the factors involved:

- feeling good physically
- being able to think clearly and problem solve without undue struggle or frustration
- feeling emotionally comfortable with oneself and others
- feeling safe in one's environment, both physically and psychologically

5. Tell the children that when they feel good physically, mentally, and emotionally and feel safe and comfortable, they can do their best thinking, feel good about themselves, get along with others, and make good decisions about their own behavior. Depending upon the age of the children, help those who picked yellow or red circles identify what they can do differently. For example, if a child is feeling physically tired, ask if he or she ate a balanced breakfast and got a good night's sleep. If the children don't want to talk about why they picked yellow or red, invite them to talk to you about it later. Then make sure you follow up with them.

6. Once the causes of imbalance have been identified for a specific child, have the child write down on the corresponding colored circle what choice/s he or she can make to help bring about a more balanced state. Parents should be involved when appropriate.

7. You might do this activity periodically to get the children used to checking in with themselves and making choices about what to change to support their own balance.

Notes

Activity 6

Options for Balancing

Purpose of this activity: When children and adults are in a state of balance, their bodies, minds, and hearts can function at optimal levels for learning and well-being. The purpose of this activity is for children to gain experience working in cooperative groups to help increase their social skills, while at the same time gaining a greater understanding of the options available for living a more balanced lifestyle. (If you haven't already done so, you might want to have the children do the activities in the beginning of this book before you do this one. That way, they will understand the concept of balance and can more easily come up with choices they can make to create balance in their lives.)

Timeframe: about 30 minutes

What you need: paper, writing utensils, and multiple copies of the letters B, A, L, N, C, and E on small slips of paper (Divide the number in your group by six, and make that many of each letter.)

What to do:

1. Introduce this activity to the children by telling them that during the next half hour they will be working in groups. Their goal is to discover the many choices they have to help themselves stay in balance so they can learn better and feel healthy as well as discover the choices they have to rebalance when things aren't going well for them. Depending on the children's understanding of the meaning of balance and its importance in their lives, you may need to spend a few minutes talking about balance and what it means to have options or choices. Remind the children that balance involves the body, mind, and heart (emotions). It also involves their interactions with others (social). If appropriate for your setting, you may add the spiritual dimension.

2. Explain to the children that the goal for this activity is for each group to come up with as many options, or choices, as possible that begin with the letter assigned to their group. They will have 10 minutes to do this. Suggest that they choose one person to facilitate the discussion and one person to record the group members' responses. Next, randomly pass out the slips of papers with letters until everyone has a letter. Tell the children that all together the letters spell the word BALANCE. (You will have only one A group, however.)

3. Explain that everyone that has a B will work together as a group, everyone with an A will be in another group, etc. Each member of the group is to come up with as many activities as possible that will help a person live a more balanced life. Each activity is to begin with the letter that the group has been assigned. Examples of activities might include:

    B: biking for physical exercise
    A: acting in a play for creativity and social relationships
    L: learning something new for mental stimulation and stimulation of the senses
    N: napping when you're tired to rest your body and mind
    C: calling a friend to get together
    E: eating a nutritious meal for a healthy body and mind

    To give the children more flexibility, you can allow them to use nouns as well as verbs, such as **Balls** to play with for exercise, **A**pples to eat for nutrition, **C**rossword puzzles to exercise the mind, and so forth.

Note: Vary your examples to fit the age group of the children. With young children, you may have to do this activity in one group, helping the children to come up with ideas by prompting them with questions.

4. After the groups have worked for about 10 minutes, ask them to stop and join each other in a circle or other arrangement suited to the size of your group. Ask the recorder from each group to share the activities the group members listed for their assigned letter. Encourage all the children to listen carefully to each recorder and to think of the activities they might want to try or add to their daily routine.

5. After all the presentations have been given, have each child choose one activity they will try within the next two days. Encourage them to think about the type of activity (physical, mental, social) that would help bring more balance into their lives.

6. Make a master list of all the groups' responses, and post it in a location that the children can see as a reminder. This could be an ongoing project for a week, two weeks, or however long you wish, depending on the children's needs and interests.

Notes

Activity 7

Cooperative Learning About Balance

Purpose of this activity: Cooperative learning is a process for developing social skills. The purpose of this activity is to help children learn the social skills of taking turns, listening and talking with others, and being members of a task team, while gaining more insights about the concept of balance.

Timeframe: about 30-45 minutes (for older children, possibly one hour)

What you need: paper, writing utensils, scissors, and magazines containing pictures of people, animals, and scenery; a poster with the bolded social skills in #3 (below) listed on it, created ahead of time using markers so it can be seen by all; a copy of Appendix Activity sheet 7 for each child

What to do:

1. Start this activity by explaining or reviewing the nature of balance and how we can become more aware of behaviors that signal balance and behaviors that signal imbalance. (For this activity, you can define balance as: a) feeling good and energetic physically, b) feeling positive about yourself, others, and your environment, and c) being able to think clearly, solve problems, and make decisions that are good for yourself and others.)

2. Ask the children what physical behaviors, emotional behaviors (facial gestures, body language, words, or behaviors that indicate particular emotions, such as laughing or crying), and mental (thinking) behaviors might show that someone is responding or acting in a balanced way. Then, ask the children to give examples of someone responding or acting in an imbalanced way. For example:

	Behaviors Indicating Balance	**Behaviors Indicating Imbalance**
Physical	Can move and play with energy	Moves sluggishly
Emotional	Has a smiling or peaceful face	Has a frown or a discouraged look
Mental	Has a positive, "can-do" attitude	Has a negative, "can't-do" attitude

3. Explain to the children that today they are going to work in groups to help them become more aware of behaviors associated with balance and imbalance. Tell them that, as they work in their groups, it's important for each group member to:

   - **listen** carefully to other members when they are giving their ideas;
   - **take turns** so that everyone can have a chance to speak;
   - **cooperate** with the other members to complete the group task; and
   - **participate** in the group by sharing their ideas and supporting the ideas of others.

4. Assign each child to a task group by having them number off from one to four or five, so each group has no more than five children in it. Assign each group a space in which to work, then ask one member from each group to pick up paper, writing utensils, scissors, and two or three magazines for his or her group.

5. Tell the groups to choose someone in each group to label one sheet of paper "In Balance" and label the second sheet of paper "Out of Balance." Then, ask the groups to brainstorm as many behaviors as they can for each of the above categories and record them on the corresponding sheet of paper. (For younger children, you may want to give each group a list of behaviors and have the children sort the items on the list by category.)

6. Tell the children that when they run out of ideas for behaviors to list, they are to look for pictures in the magazines that show balanced and imbalanced behaviors. Ask them to cut out the pictures and put them with the corresponding list of behaviors. Remind the children to work as a team and to listen, take turns, cooperate, and participate. That way, they will be more successful and have more fun doing the task.

7. Check with the groups, and when most or all of them have exhausted their ideas and pictures of behaviors, ask each group to designate one person to share the group's ideas and pictures with the entire group of children.

8. Now give each child an Appendix Activity 7 sheet, and ask the children to rate themselves on the social skills listed on the sheet (those in #3 and on the poster), using the following scale (given on the sheet):

    1 (did well)
    2 (did okay)
    3 (needs improvement)

    They needn't put their names on their papers.

9. After the children have rated themselves, have them circle the social skills for which they rated themselves 3. Collect their papers and tabulate the frequency of all the social skills that were rated 3. Save this tabulation until the next time you do a cooperative learning experience with the children, reminding them to pay special attention to any social-skill behaviors that were rated 3, so they can improve on these each time they work in a group.

    You also might call their attention to the fact that these same social skills are very important in being a friend as well as in any other social relationship.

10. Finally, ask the children to volunteer any ideas about how they can use what they learned from doing this activity in their daily lives.

Notes

Section 2

Achieving Balance Through Meeting the Needs of the Body, Mind, and Heart

Activity 8

Body, Mind, and Heart

Purpose of this activity: We tend to think of the body, the mind, and the heart (feelings) as separate parts of us that perform entirely different functions. This activity is meant to increase children's awareness of how much the functions of moving and resting (body), thinking (mind), and feeling (heart), are entertwined. This knowledge can help them understand the value of balance between the body, mind, and heart.

Timeframe: about 20 minutes for young children and about 45 minutes for older children, depending on how long the discussion extends

What you need: pictures of people engaged in moving and resting, thinking, and feeling (one picture for each of the three); a flipchart or poster board; pencils, crayons or markers, and one sheet of paper per child

What to do:

1. Before you begin this activity with the children, place on a flipchart or poster board pictures that represent people engaged in moving or resting, thinking, and showing feelings. Next to each picture place the corresponding statements:

    My body helps me move and rest.
    My mind helps me think.
    My heart helps me feel.

    Place the flipchart or poster in a location that is easily visible to all of the children.

2. Distribute paper, pencils, and drawing tools to each child. Ask the children to either:

    *   draw an object, person, or animal,
    *   make a design using a variety of colors, or
    *   choose something within the room to observe and draw.

    Depending on the age of the children, this part of the activity can take from 5 to 15 minutes.

3. At the conclusion of #2, have the children share how their bodies (through movement) helped them in this drawing activity, how their minds (thinking) helped them, and how their hearts (feelings) helped them. You might also ask them:

    When you're drawing a picture, what difference do you think it would make if you had a stomachache or if you were really tired?

    When you're drawing a picture, what difference do you think it would make if your mind were full of thoughts about other things?

When you're drawing a picture, what difference do you think it would make if you were feeling really angry about something?

4. For younger children, conclude this activity by pointing out that our minds, hearts, and bodies are so connected that they all have an effect on each other as well as on everything we do. This is true whether our bodies, minds, and hearts are active or peaceful and resting.

5. For older children, you could write the following thought-provoking questions on the flipchart or poster board (or chalk- or whiteboard):

    Can we move or rest without thinking and feeling?
    Can we think without feeling and moving?
    Can we feel without thinking and moving?

    On the back side of their drawing paper, have each child write yes, no, or maybe for each of the three questions. Then, have the children share their answers with the person to their left and give the reasons for their answers.

    For each question, ask for a show of hands to determine the number of children who said yes, no, or maybe, and record the numbers. Ask for volunteers to share their answers and reasoning with the whole group.

    Tell them that these questions may have different answers depending on how you look at them, but they are interesting to consider.

6. Discuss the fact that the body, mind, and heart affect each other but that each plays a different role in how we conduct our daily lives at home, in our neighborhoods, and in learning and being with others at school.

    Point out that even when the body, mind, or heart is—or seems to be—inactive, it is affecting the other two. For example, sometimes we can do our best thinking when our feelings are neutral, and we can feel very peaceful when our minds and bodies are quiet. Also, there are times when we "act without thinking." If we are acting out of strong emotions, or feelings, we might do something we later regret. On the other hand, people sometimes do heroic acts without thinking, when they act out of instinct, or "gut feelings." You might want to ask the children what they think about gut feelings. Why are they called "gut" feelings? Are they connected with our bodies? Are they connected with our minds? Are they really feelings?

7. Ask what the children have learned from this activity and discussion about the body, mind, and heart. How will their new awareness change the way they think, feel, or act in the world?

Notes

Activity 9

Our Five Senses as Gateways to the World

Purpose of this activity: Observation is key to whatever we do. Our eyes, ears, nose, mouth, and skin provide us with our senses of sight, hearing, smell, taste, and touch. They are the physical gateways through which we learn about, interact with, and enjoy the world. The purpose of this activity is to increase the children's awareness of and appreciation for their five physical senses. With awareness usually comes more active use of all the senses and thus a balance between them.

(If you have children in your class or group who have one or more impaired senses, be sure to emphasize that human beings are amazing in their ability to adapt to such situations by more fully developing the senses they do have. You might want to discuss Helen Keller or read a book about this resourceful woman. In addition, you could mention that humans can also use the nonphysical senses they have, such as "gut feelings," or intuition—knowing something without knowing how you know. This might lead to a very interesting discussion in itself.)

Timeframe: one hour (If you don't have an hour, you can do one or more of the separate components of this activity with the option to extend this activity over five days, as explained in #5 and #6 below.)

What you need: a pencil and writing paper for each child and a variety of objects that the children can explore with their senses. Be sure to include things with a variety of shapes, sizes, colors, aromas, sounds, textures, and tastes (if you can arrange for them to safely taste things in your situation).

What to do:

1. Introduce the five senses as structures of the body that provide gateways for us to learn about, interact with, and enjoy the world around us. Then, allow about five minutes for the discussion of each one. Help the children brainstorm all the ways they can think of that each sense helps us learn about the people, animal and plant life, objects, experiences, and events around us. List these on a flipchart.

2. Have a variety of objects on a table, and ask the children to come and each take an object to observe. The idea is to use as many senses as you can and write down everything you observe about the object. Then take the object back to the table and choose another to observe. (To include taste, you could have bowls of raisins, grapes or cherries, small carrots, or salty crackers, for example. Each child could take one and write down what it looks, feels, smells, and tastes like. If they are really observant, they might record that crackers makes crunchy sounds when they eat them. In this case, the children would not return the objects to the bowls!)

    When each child has had the opportunity to record observations on a few objects (decide how many given your available time), stop and ask for volunteers to share what they have written. Did they include all possible senses for each object? Did they record color, shape, size (approximate, such as tiny, small, medium-sized, or large, given what they could determine by "eyeballing" or feeling the object), texture, smell, and taste (if appropriate)?

3. Now that the function and importance of each of the body's gateways have been established, have the children write down or sketch what they do to take care of each of the gateways. (See also

Activity 12, The Eyes Have It!) Examples are: keeping the skin clean, sleeping to rest the eyes or wearing sunglasses to protect them, cleaning the ears, taking vitamins and eating right, going to the doctor for checkups.

4. Have each child share their responses to #3 with a partner, or do a group sharing of the responses.

5. If you choose to extend the activity, keep the lists from #1 posted in a place the children can see them each morning for another five days. Ask the children to be conscious of how they use their five senses at home. Sometime each morning take a few minutes to add additional insights to the original data gathered in #1. The number and types of ideas generated will largely depend upon the ages of the children. Encourage children to share these ideas with other people in their lives and ask for additional ideas.

6. If you extend the activity, for each of the five days you have the children explore their senses, designate a gateway to consciously appreciate and do something nice for that gateway. For example, for the ears, listen to some fun or peaceful music. For the nose, smell some flowers or other pleasant aromas. For the eyes, stop what you are doing and rest your eyes by closing them for a few moments—or look out the window at the trees and sky to refresh them. For the skin, take a shower and feel the water on your skin, or wear something fuzzy or smooth next to your skin.

Notes

Activity 10

Stop, Look, and Listen

Purpose of this activity: Observation is key to our gaining awareness of the world around us, which, in turn, affects how we feel and the actions we take. To become better observers, we need to slow down and take in what we sense or feel, what we see, hear, touch, and smell. The purpose of this activity is to increase children's observation skills for sensing and feeling, seeing, and hearing.

Timeframe: about 30 minutes

What you need: paper and writing and drawing utensils

What to do:

1. Have the children sit somewhere comfortable where they can write and draw, and give them paper and writing and drawing utensils.

2. Ask them to close their eyes and tune in to what they are sensing or feeling in the moment. Then, have them open their eyes and record in a few words or a drawing what they sensed or felt.

3. Next, have them look around them, above them, and below them. Ask them to note or draw what they saw in as much detail as they can.

4. Then, ask the children to close their eyes again and focus on the sounds they hear. Once more, have them record the sources of the sounds in writing or drawing.

5. Have each child share with a neighbor (or to the whole group, if time allows) what they discovered by becoming "observers of the moment."

6. Discuss the value of using the skills of observation in our everyday lives. Ask the children to do the above activity on their own in an environment of their choosing, which might be home, the neighborhood, a shopping mall, or a place in nature. Set a date for them to report back on their observations.

7. Suggest that the children take time each day to stop, look, and listen.

Notes

Activity 11

Five-Minute Version of Stop, Look, Listen

Purpose of this activity: This five-minute activity helps children practice their observation skills of sensing, feeling, seeing, and listening. It also helps them ground, center, and focus themselves, and it helps them practice remembering and describing their observations.

Timeframe: five minutes

What you need: no materials needed

What to do:

1. Use the cue "Stop, Look, Listen!" whenever you want the children to do this spontaneous activity. Explain the following procedure ahead of time.

2. First, the children are to stop whatever they are doing and either sit or stand quietly in place. Ask them, "What do you feel?" They have one minute to identify what they are sensing or feeling in their bodies at this moment. Tell them to remember their feelings and sensations. Let them know when the minute is up.

3. Then tell the children to take one minute to look around, above, and below them. Ask them, "What do you see?" Tell them to remember four things they saw. Let them know when the minute is up.

4. Finally, ask the children to close their eyes for one minute and listen to the sounds they hear around them. Ask them, "What do you hear?" Tell them to remember what they hear. Let them know when the minute is up.

5. Take two minutes and ask for volunteers to share what they sensed or felt, saw, and heard.

6. Encourage the children to do this activity on their own in a number of different settings to see what new information they can learn about their various environments.

Notes

Activity 12

The Eyes Have It!

Purpose of this activity: So much of what we take in about the world around us is taken in through the eyes. This activity promotes the awareness of how much we use our eyes to learn and understand what is taking place in our various environments. It also encourages taking good care of these magnificent tools for exploration and discovery.

Timeframe: 30-45 minutes

What you need: an environment of your choice

What to do:

1. Have the children gather in an environment that can be either indoors or outdoors.

2. Have them close their eyes and think about what is around them without looking. What are the people next to them wearing? What is above them? Below them? What objects are around them? How big are they? What colors are they? How many people are in the space? What is on the walls (if they are inside)? What is in the distance (if they are outside)? Have them guess all these answers, if they can. Have them take two or three steps with their eyes closed.

3. Now have the children open their eyes. Ask a few volunteers to share what they experienced during this exercise. How did it feel to be unable to see what was around them? To move with their eyes closed?

4. Next, ask the children to slowly and quietly move about this space for about five minutes. (If you are outside rather than in a room, define the boundary.) Encourage them to observe the general nature of the space and the people, objects, and colors they see as they move about.

5. When the five minutes are up, have the children join you in a circle and get seated comfortably. Ask them how it felt to be able to use their eyes now. How was it different from when their eyes were closed? Have each person decide on one observation to share with the rest of the children.

6. Thank the children for their observations, and emphasize the importance of our eyes as gateways to the world around us.

7. Ask them to share ways they can take care of and protect their eyes (e.g., wearing sunglasses or goggles when circumstances call for it, eating nutritiously to nourish the eyes, getting enough sleep, not sitting too close to the television and not watching too much of it, doing activities that require both near and far vision, looking away or closing the eyes occasionally when doing close-up work to rest the eyes).

8. Remind the children to use their eyes to their best advantage by carefully observing what is around them to expand their experiences of the world.

Notes

Activity 13

Creating a Sound Collage

Purpose of this activity: We are constantly surrounded by sounds, some of which are pleasant and some of which are disturbing or create a feeling of discomfort in the body, mind, and heart. Pleasant, comfortable sounds help us feel alive and peaceful (or balanced), whereas discordant sounds can make us feel restless or anxious. Feeling this way puts stress on our bodies, minds, and hearts. The purpose of this activity is to help children become more aware of the sounds in their various environments and how these sounds affect them.

Timeframe: about 45 minutes

What you need: sheets of poster board or heavy paper; magazines to cut up that include a variety of pictures of people, animals, and objects; glue or paste; scissors for each child; markers or crayons

What to do:

1. Introduce this activity to the children by having them close their eyes, take a few deep breaths, and relax their bodies by imagining they are sitting on soft grass by a lake.

2. Ask the children to be very quiet and listen to all the sounds in the room and surrounding environment. Have them picture in their minds the location of each sound. Is it in the room? What part of the room? Is it coming from the hallway, the yard outside the window, or the road? Also, have them picture in their minds the sources of the sounds, such as a fan, fluorescent lights, a person, an animal, an airplane, a car, or a machine. (If you are in a very quiet room, you might want to take time before this activity to record some sounds in various environments, then play the recording for the children.)

3. Next, have the children open their eyes and check the sources of the sounds visually. Pass out magazines, and have them look for pictures of the sources of the sounds they heard. If they can't find pictures of some sources, they may wish to draw the pictures. If they can't find the right pictures and don't know how to draw the sources, allow them to use words along with pictures and drawings. Have them cut out and paste their pictures on sheets of poster board or other heavy paper and add drawings and words, if they wish.

4. Explain to the children that they are creating a "sound collage." If the children are not familiar with what a collage is, you can explain that it is a single piece of artwork made up of many smaller pieces that represent an idea.

5. When the children finish putting representations on their poster boards for all the sounds they heard, have them remember and focus on one sound at a time. Ask them to sense how that sound felt in their bodies. Was it relaxing, or did it make them feel uncomfortable? Then ask how it affected their thinking. Did it help them focus and calm their minds, or did it make their thoughts come faster and jump around more? Ask if the sound made a difference in the rhythm of their heartbeats, either speeding them up or slowing them down. If they don't know, have them guess.

6. If the sound had a positive effect on them, instruct them to draw a circle in their favorite color around the picture, drawing, or word. If the sound had a negative effect on them, have them choose a color they don't like and make an X through the picture, drawing, or word.

7. Have the children think about how their sound collages help them become more aware of the effects that sounds have on their bodies, minds, and hearts. Ask for volunteers to share ideas about how to bring more positive sounds into their various environments and how to decrease or eliminate sounds that have negative effects. You may want to start by discussing the sounds in the present room and surroundings, and then extend the ideas to other environments.

Notes

Activity 14

Breathing for Balance

Purpose of this activity: Breathing adequate, clean air is basic to human survival. We can live a few weeks without food and a few days without water, but only a few minutes without oxygen. The purpose of this activity is to increase children's awareness of how important it is for their overall health and learning to breathe in enough good quality air and to help them breathe most effectively.

Timeframe: about 15 to 30 minutes

What you need: a comfortable space in which the children can stand, sit, or lie down

What to do:

1. Begin this activity by having the children find a comfortable space to sit within a defined space in either random or circular order. Start the discussion by asking the question "Why do we need to breathe?" Lead the children to the conclusion that we need to breathe in order to take in oxygen from the air, which is necessary for us to stay alive.

2. Have the children silently observe their breathing patterns for about one minute by paying attention to their in-breaths (inhales) and their out-breaths (exhales). Then have them place the left hand on the part of the body where they feel the breath is going to and leaving from as it travels back out of the body. For most children, this will be either the chest area or the lower abdominal area, just below the navel.

3. Point out that we can take in the most air and receive the most benefit from our breathing if we breathe from the lower abdominal, or belly, area. By breathing from this area, we take in the most oxygen and give out the most carbon dioxide, a waste product of our bodies. Have the children practice breathing from this area by having them place both hands on the lower abdominal area and then take in air to the count of three and exhale to the count of three. Do this slowly and rhythmically by counting out loud in unison for two or three minutes.

4. Ask the children to stand and continue breathing with their hands on the lower bellies, paying attention to the movement of their hands in and out as they breathe. Most children should feel an expansion (belly and hands moving outward) on the inhale and a contraction (belly and hands moving inward) on the exhale. Have younger children, and others when appropriate, lie on their backs on the floor. Again, have them place their hands on the lower abdominal area and feel and watch their hands rise on an inhale and sink on an exhale. Depending on available time and the children, you can have each child place a lightweight book on his or her belly and observe the book going up and down.

    If any of the children have a baby sister or brother, ask them to observe how the baby breathes, as babies naturally breathe from this area of their bodies.

5. To further their understanding of the importance of taking deep breaths from the lower abdominal area, call the children's attention to the following facts:

- Our bodies can survive only a few minutes without oxygen.

- Our brains, which weigh about three pounds when fully developed, consume about 20 percent of the body's oxygen, so oxygen is necessary for thinking and learning.

- The body needs oxygen to convert food into the energy it needs for all of its functions.

- The oxygen in our bodies must be replaced every moment to support our health, learning, and actions.

- Stress is very hard on our bodies, minds, and emotions. Breathing deeply helps reduce stress.

Add other facts as appropriate for the ages of the children involved.

6. End this activity by asking the children what they learned by doing this activity.

7. Encourage the children to stop occasionally during their daily activities to take a few deep breaths. Let them know that this is especially helpful if they are feeling low on energy, stressed out, upset, or anxious.

Note: The breathing part of this activity can be revisited at any time, and especially those times when children need support to relax, become more focused, and achieve a more balanced state of being.

Notes

Activity 15

Stop, Breathe, Two, Three

Purpose of this activity: Taking deep breaths brings more oxygen into our minds and bodies and helps release tension. The purpose of this activity is to teach children a way to revitalize their minds and bodies through taking deep breaths.

Timeframe: five minutes or less

What you need: a comfortable place for the children to stand

What to do:

1. Have the children stop whatever they are doing and find a comfortable place to stand.

2. Ask the children to place their hands, one on top of the other, about 2 inches below their navels. Remind them that our deepest and most beneficial breathing happens when we breathe from this area.

3. Focusing the children's attention on the hand area of their abdomens, have them inhale a deep breath. Most of the children will feel this area expand by feeling a slight pushing against their hands as they take deep breaths. Then, have the children exhale, feeling their hands move in slightly.

4. Vary the breathing rhythm by having the children take an in-breath to the count of three or four and an out-breath to a count of six or seven, letting out all the breath possible.

5. Explain that breathing this way will, oddly enough, bring both more energy and more relaxation to the body as well as focus to the mind. Encourage them to do this type of breathing whenever they want to feel more energized, relaxed, and focused. Then, with revitalized minds and bodies, have the children return to what they were doing.

Notes

Activity 16

Drinking Water as a Habit

Purpose of this activity: The body, brain, and heart need to be well hydrated in order to carry out their functions efficiently. The purpose of this activity is to have children assess how much water they drink on a daily basis and to become more aware of the importance of drinking water to support their body, brain, and heart functions for learning and well-being.

Timeframe: about 15 minutes

What you need: a chalkboard, flipchart, or poster board with appropriate drawing utensils; writing or drawing paper and writing or drawing utensils for the children

What to do:

1. On a piece of writing or drawing paper, have each child write the number or draw the number of glasses of water they think they drink each day. Then, using a different color, write down or draw the number of bottles or glasses of soft drink (soda pop) they consume each day. Using other colors, have the children record additional beverages they consume on a daily basis, such as milk and juice. (If you think it's necessary, you may want to have the children keep track of this consumption for a week before doing this activity. This, in itself, will create an awareness.)

2. By a show of hands, have the children indicate the number of glasses of water each consumes every day by starting with 10 or higher, recording the number of hands, and then counting downward. Do the same procedure for soda pop, milk, and any other beverages consumed on a daily basis, counting glasses, bottles, or cans. Create a simple bar graph of the number of glasses of each kind of beverage consumed by the children. Following is a hypothetical example.

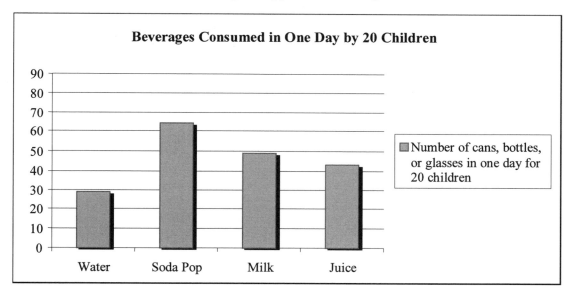

3. Have the children share what they think their bodies and minds get from water, soda pop, milk, and juice (or whatever beverages they mentioned). Lead them to the conclusion that the body and mind need water for survival and efficient functioning. Share the fact that water makes up about 70 percent of the body's composition. We can live only days if we are deprived of water.

Although soda pop has some water in it, otherwise it has no value for the body, and in large quantities is harmful due to excess sugar, caffeine, and artificial ingredients. Diet pop can actually make people gain weight, because it stimulates the taste buds without providing nutrients and thus creates the urge to eat.

The body obtains beneficial food nutrients from milk, such as calcium, protein, and vitamins A, C, and D. Encourage the children to talk with their parents about their need for these nutrients. If milk and dairy products cause allergic reactions in a child, he or she can explore substituting soy or almond milk for regular milk.

Juice (depending on the kind and amount of actual fruit juice in it) has some nutritional value, but often it is largely sugar and water mixed with a little fruit juice. The sugar content of pop and juice is generally so high that it should be consumed in moderation. Excess consumption of sugar is harmful to a person's health and can fog the mind, making it more difficult to concentrate and learn. Sugar consumption creates temporary energy spikes that are followed by lows, thus creating an imbalance in the body's energy.

4. Ask the children to each make a goal of developing the habit of drinking about six to eight glasses of water a day (more if in warm climates and/or engaging in a lot of physical activity), and, if drinking pop every day, substitute water for pop, reserving pop for an occasional treat.

5. Remind the children about drinking water periodically, and chart their consumption again after a while to see how it has changed. You might want to extend this activity and have the children search out further facts about how the body and brain use water.

"Children are not educated to drink water; they become dependent on sodas and juices. This is a self-imposed restriction on the water needs of the body. It is not generally possible to drink manufactured beverages in full replacement of the water needs of the body. At the same time, a cultivated preference for the taste of these sodas will automatically reduce the free urge to drink water when sodas are not available."

F. Batmanghelidj, M.D., *Your Body's Many Cries for Water*

Notes

Activity 17

The Many Colors of Healthy Food

Purpose of this activity: This activity is meant to raise children's awareness about the variety of foods available to nourish their bodies. The theme of the activity is the colors of foods, as color is a concrete, visible aspect to which children can relate. Eating foods in a variety of different colors is one way to ensure getting the many different nutrients the body needs.

Timeframe: about 45 minutes to one hour

What you need: one copy for each child of the Activity 8, Food Colors Bar Graph, in the Appendix; crayons or markers in a variety of colors; one poster board and markers that you can use to combine the children's results into a graph for the wall

What to do:

1. Begin by discussing food with the children. Ask them to think about the different foods they've eaten lately. What colors were those foods? Ask a few volunteers to give examples (e.g., peas—green; strawberries—red). Explain that eating foods in a variety of different colors is one way to help yourself get the different vitamins and minerals and other nutrients your body needs to work right and be strong and healthy.

2. Tell the children they are now going to see how many different foods they can think of and record the colors of those foods on a Food Colors Bar Graph. If they don't understand the concept of a bar graph, now is a good time to explain that it is a way to make a picture of how different things compare to each other. In this case, the highest bar will be the color found most in foods they know. Ask if they can guess what color that will be. Tell them they'll find out which color "wins" (i.e., which bar is the highest) when they get their graphs finished and you combine everyone's graph into one. (For young children, you can do just the one large graph given their verbal input and a little prompting.)

3. Give each child a copy of Appendix Activity 8, Food Colors Bar Graph, and crayons or markers.

4. Show them that some colors are listed along the bottom of the graph and numbers from 1 to 12 go up the left side. Their instructions are to a) write the names of foods under their respective colors, and b) for each food, color a box that color above the color name. For example, "red" might have "strawberry" written below it and a red box colored in above it. The more foods they list under a particular color, the more boxes they can fill in for that color, and the higher that color's bar will be.

   For a white food, they can use black and trace the outline of one of the squares above "white." Explain that "brown" means anywhere from tan to dark brown. Some foods might come in more than one color (e.g., peppers), so those foods can be listed under all their colors, but only the color of the edible part can be listed. (E.g., a watermelon is green on the outside, but we eat the red part, so it would be listed under red. Similarly, don't count stems or leaves or other parts that aren't eaten.) Also, tell them to list single foods and not foods that have more than one ingredient, such as pizza.

5. Give the children about 15-20 minutes to think about and color their graphs. (Adjust time to your group and schedule.)

6. While they are working, prepare a blank graph on your poster board (or use a whiteboard). When the time is up, ask the children to share their results, taking turns with volunteers. Start with one color, and color in the large graph until all foods they've listed on their own graphs have been recorded. Look to see which color "won." Did they guess it correctly?

7. Remind the children that the more colors they can eat, the more they are likely to get what they need from food to be healthy.

8. If you want to extend this activity, tell the children that now they have discovered which color is found the most in foods they know about—but people around the world eat many foods that are unfamiliar to us. And even our own grocery stores have foods that perhaps we have never eaten. Ask them if they have ever eaten foods such as the following:

    kiwi (fruit that's green on the inside with little black seeds and has a brown fuzzy outside)
    star fruit (fruit that's yellow on the inside and is shaped like a star when sliced)
    rutabaga (yellowish root vegetable)
    eggplant (fruit that's dark purple outside, off-white inside)
    mango (fruit that can be green, yellow, and red outside and is yellow-orange inside)
    papaya (fruit that's green outside, yellow inside)
    fresh coconut (fruit, the nut of which is white inside)
    tofu (white, made of soybeans)
    turnip (white root vegetable)
    artichoke (green vegetable that is really the immature flowerhead of a plant)
    pomegranate (large, reddish berry the size of an orange)
    persimmon (orange berry)
    leek (green vegetable)
    others …

    You may want to have some unusual foods on hand to show the children.

9. Tell the children to look carefully around the supermarket at all the colors and kinds of foods in the produce department the next time they are there. Perhaps they could try a new kind of fruit or vegetable. Maybe a colorful one.

10. Have the children imagine as they eat their different foods how the nutrients in those foods are giving them strong bodies, energy to run and play, and clear minds to think well. Tell them to silently thank their food for keeping them alive and healthy!

List of Possible Foods for an Expanded Food Bar Graph

You may wish to do a larger Food Bar Graph with the children, adding more colors and more foods.

apples (red, yellow, green)	meats (color raw or when cooked to eat)
apricots	milk
asparagus	mushrooms
bananas	nectarines
beans (different kinds, such as green beans, lima beans, baked beans, butter beans, kidney beans)	nuts
	onion
	oranges
beets	peaches
blackberries	pears
black-eyed peas	peas
blueberries	peppers (green, yellow, red)
brussels sprouts	pineapple
cabbage	plums
cantaloupe	potatoes
cauliflower	prunes
celery	raisins
cheese	raspberries
cherries	seeds
cucumbers	spinach
eggs	squash
figs	strawberries
fish (ex., salmon—pink)	sweet potatoes
grains	tomatoes
grapefruit	watermelon
grapes	white rice
lemons	wild rice
lettuce	yams
limes	zucchini

Notes

Activity 18

Food-O! Game

Purpose of this activity: Good nutrition is more likely to be achieved when a person eats a wide variety of foods. Children often are not aware of the many food choices available, as they aren't the ones who do the grocery shopping and cooking. This activity is a game to acquaint children with foods that come from plants and whether they are roots, stems, leaves, fruits, flowers (florets), nuts, or seeds. The ultimate purpose of the activity is to encourage the children to include foods from all these categories in their diets, thus providing their bodies with a balance of nutrients for health. Awareness is half the battle.

Timeframe: about 45 minutes but can be shortened or extended to fit the time available

What you need: Appendix Activity 9 game board and cards and heavy white paper or lightweight cardstock on which to copy them. Two versions are provided—a simple one with picture cards for young children and a bigger one with word cards for older children. You'll need one game board per child and enough cards (copied and cut out) to give 15 picture cards to each young child or 25 word cards to each older child. (The cards will be randomly chosen from a pile of all food categories combined.)

The first time (or first few times) you play the game, the children probably will not know the categories of all the foods. (Many adults may not either!) If you want to help them out, you can give each of the young children who can read paper copies of the two pictorial game card sheets, which list the categories by rows down at the bottom. For the word version, you may give each of the older children a copy of the sheet listing the foods by their categories (also in the Appendix). Even this longer list is by no means all-inclusive, and you may want to add to either list.

What to do:

1. Introduce the game by telling the children that today they will learn about plants that provide us with food and have fun playing the Food-O! game. Explain that we get food from various parts of plants, including roots, stems, leaves, fruits, flowers (florets), nuts, and seeds. Plants give us a variety of nutrients, and the more different plant parts we eat, the more likely we will get what we need to be healthy.

2. Give each child the appropriate game board and cards. You may either have them choose their own cards randomly from a box, or count out and give each child cards that you randomly choose from the box. If this is the first time you have played the game, give them each a copy of the appropriate food list for the age group. (The longer list is below as well as in the Appendix.)

3. The object of the game is to see who can be the first to fill one row of boxes on the game board with cards. (You may have multiple winners, which is fine. The idea here is to learn more than it is to compete.) A row may be filled vertically, horizontally, or diagonally (a good chance to learn those words, if they don't know them).

4. Tell the children you are going to call out a square (i.e., B3) and, initially, show them how to locate that square. You will then say a plant part (i.e., root, stem, etc.), and they must find a card with a food in that category and put it on that square. You will keep calling out squares and parts until someone has completed a row and raises his or her hand and says "Food-O!" (Keep track of the

squares and parts you call on a game board, and if you call all the squares and no one has completed a row, see who has the most squares in a row filled. Check to make sure they have filled the squares correctly with foods in the categories you called.)

The first time (or few times) you play the game, you may want to allow the children to use their category lists to determine the categories of the foods on their cards. Later, if you want to make the game more of a challenge, play it without the lists. The list below is the same as the word list in Appendix Activity 9.

5. After you play the game and the children are more familiar with the foods and categories, suggest that they take the category list home and become more aware of what parts of plants they are eating each day. The list might spark discussion and new food adventures in their families, too!

Categories of Foods from Plants

Roots	Fruit	Flower Buds (Florets)
beet	apple	artichoke
carrot	avocado	broccoli
parsnip	blackberry	cauliflower
potato	blueberry	
radish	cantaloupe	**Nuts**
rutabaga	cranberry	almond
turnip	cucumber	coconut
yam	kumquat	filbert
	currant	macadamia
Stems	eggplant	peanut
asparagus	mango	pecan
celery	nectarine	walnut
kohlrabi	orange	
rhubarb	papaya	**Seeds**
	peach	bean
Leaves	pear	corn
cabbage	pineapple	millet
endive	plum	oats
lettuce	raspberry	pea
parsley	strawberry	pine nut
spinach	tomato	quinoa (keenwah)
dandelion greens	watermelon	rice
		soybean
		wheat

Notes

Activity 19

What's for Breakfast?

Purpose of this activity: Eating a balanced breakfast that includes protein, carbohydrates, and "good" fats is important for learning and well-being. The purpose of this activity is to help children become aware of what a balanced breakfast is and the value of eating a good breakfast for better learning and appropriate behaviors.

Timeframe: about 30-45 minutes

What you need: empty containers of breakfast items, pictures of breakfast items, and/or magazines containing pictures of breakfast items, and one copy of Appendix Activity 10 for each child

What to do:

1. Place the materials needed for this activity in a central location accessible to all of the children.

2. Make the statement: "What you eat for breakfast either helps or gets in the way of your learning and well-being." Ask all those who think this statement is true to line up to the right of you and all those who think that what they eat for breakfast doesn't make a difference line up to the left of you.

3. Have each line of children form into groups of three or four depending upon the total number of children present. Have the group members take turns telling their groups what they usually eat for breakfast. One member from each group will then go and choose a container or picture for each of the items mentioned by their group members. Older children can cut out pictures from magazines for this part.

4. Have the children who agreed with your initial statement and the children who didn't compare the breakfast items they have chosen. Have them note the similarities and differences to determine if thinking that breakfast is important affects their choices of what they eat for breakfast. If there are any children who skip breakfast, encourage them to listen to what the other children have to say.

5. Next, introduce the concept that a balanced breakfast includes a food (or foods) high in protein (e.g., eggs, peanut butter, meat), whole grain bread or cereal, a fruit or vegetable, a small amount of fat, and milk or yogurt.

    You might discuss that fat is often included with the protein component. You can also mention that white bread is not whole grain. Depending on the age of the children, suggest they begin to read labels to see if their breads and cereals are whole grain.

6. Then, have each group of children check the items that represent what they generally eat for breakfast compared to the food items included in a balanced breakfast. Congratulate the children who discover that they are eating a balanced breakfast. Encourage the children who are skipping breakfast or not eating a balanced breakfast to choose a balanced variety of food to start their days. Ask them to try their new choices for the next week and note how their bodies feel and if it is easier for them to concentrate and learn. Encourage them to use the chart form on the Appendix sheet for this activity to record what they eat for breakfast and the corresponding effects.

(You might want to send a note home to parents briefly explaining this activity and its purpose so they can be prepared to help out.)

7. Periodically remind the children to try eating a balanced breakfast, and after a week or so, have them share their experiences and how they feel.

Notes

Activity 20

Sleeping for Balance

Purpose of this activity: Sleep is necessary for our entire being. During sleep, the body, mind, and heart rest so they can be rejuvenated. Sleep allows downtime for growth and healing and for our minds to consolidate and integrate the day's learning so it can be transferred into long-term memory. Children and adults who do not get enough sleep and/or a good quality of sleep compromise their quality of life, productivity, and ability to get along with themselves and others. Insufficient or poor quality sleep results in chronic tiredness and irritability and puts stress on the body. The purpose of this activity is to introduce children to the importance of sleep in their lives and to give them options for getting more restful sleep.

Timeframe: about 15 minutes for each of the two parts

What you need: a flipchart or poster board, one small slip of paper for each child, and writing utensils

What to do:

Part 1

1. When you first meet the children, ask them: "How many of you had a good night's sleep last night?" (Give them a hint that one way to tell if they had a good night's sleep is to notice how well-rested they feel.) Have children respond by a show of hands. Count the number of yeses and noes, and record each of these numbers on the flipchart in a YES column and a NO column.

2. Ask the children to say about how many hours of sleep they thought they had. (Young children probably will not know, and if so, just skip this part, or see if they can tell you what time they went to bed and what time they got up and do the math for them.) Record any responses from the Yes group in the YES column and responses from the No group in the NO column on the flipchart. Calculate the average number of hours for each group, and compare this figure to the number of hours for their age group. Listed below are the number of hours of sleep generally recommended for the following age groups:

   - Children ages one to three generally need 10 to 12 hours.
   - Children ages four through pre-teens generally need 9 to 10 hours.
   - Teenagers generally need 8 to 9 hours.

   Talk about times to go to bed and times to arise that would give your age group enough sleep. E.g., if your children are eight and nine years old, and they get up at 6:00 in the morning, they would have to go to bed by 8:00 or 9:00 at night.

3. Have children in the NO group share comments about how they feel when they wake up and how they feel at different times of the day. Record these responses on the flipchart. Then ask the children in the YES group to share comments regarding how they feel when they wake up and throughout the day. Record these comments in the appropriate column on the flipchart.

   Compare the similarities and differences in the responses between the two groups.

4. Next, have the children brainstorm ways they can chart their hours of sleep and how they feel when they get up and throughout the day on that amount of sleep, and brainstorm ways they can get more hours of sleep if they are not getting enough.

5. At the completion of #4, have the children write down one thing they can do to help themselves get the hours of sleep they need to feel good and have the energy to do the tasks they need and want to do throughout each day.

Part 2

1. Explain to the children that in addition to needing an adequate amount of sleep, we also need to have a restful sleep in order to get the full benefits of sleeping. They may have difficulty going to sleep, they may wake up several times a night, and/or they may not get a deep sleep. Any one of these situations is like subtracting time from the total number of hours they sleep. Tell the children that doing quiet activities, listening to calming music, taking a shower or bath before bedtime, and reading happy, calming stories can all help to prepare them for a restful night's sleep.

2. After this introduction, ask for a show of hands as to how many children feel they get a restful sleep most nights. Then ask these children to share the ways they prepare for bedtime. You can record their activities or preparations on the flipchart as resources for the children who need to improve their quality of sleep. Ask if anyone has any additional ideas and offer your own.

3. On a slip of paper, have the children who need to improve their quality of sleep write down one idea that they want to try. Encourage them to note how doing this one thing before bedtime helps them. If it has no effect (or makes things worse), have them choose another idea to try. Younger children will need to engage their parents in this process.

4. After one week, ask the children again if they got enough sleep the night before, and discuss how their sleep patterns have changed to determine if progress is being made. If any children are still having problems getting enough or good quality sleep, brainstorm possible solutions again and have those children write down new strategies to try.

    Parents will need to be involved if sleep problems continue. A note home explaining your sleep "project" and listing possible strategies for better sleep that all of you have brainstormed may help immensely.

5. As the children improve their sleep patterns, note any differences in learning and behavior that occur in individual children and the group as a whole.

Notes

Activity 21

Moving Like the Animals

Purpose of this activity: Movement interspersed with sitting and focused, quiet activity supports the learning process by revitalizing the body and the mind. It is important that children be encouraged and given the opportunity to move many times a day.

Timeframe: about 15-30 minutes (and can be adapted to five minutes once the children are familiar with the movements)

What you need: an adequate floor space for movement

What to do:

1. Introduce this activity by having the children close their eyes, take a few deep breaths (from the lower abdominal area), then mentally picture one or more animals moving about in various ways in their natural habitats. Have them do this for one to three minutes, depending on the age of the children.

2. After the specified time, ask the children to open their eyes. Allow them to reflect for a few moments on how they saw the animals moving. Then ask for volunteers to share, either through words or movement, what they experienced.

3. Taking the children's ideas, ask children to volunteer to lead the other children in the movements of the animals they chose, supplementing their ideas with the following suggestions:

    Stretch like a cat.
    Act like a dog that wants to go out for a walk.
    Gallup like a horse.
    Walk like an elephant, swinging your arms like a trunk.
    Spread your wings like a bird that's getting ready to fly.
    Hop like a rabbit.
    Walk like a monkey.
    Wiggle like a snake.

4. When they finish the movements, have the children take a few deep breaths and find a comfortable place to sit. Ask for volunteers to share what they experienced during the movements. Have the children think about how they felt before they started doing the movements and how they feel now. Note the differences. Remind children that remembering to breathe deeply and engage in movement several times a day is important to feeling good and to learning more efficiently.

5. Point out that many animals count on moving quickly and easily to obtain food and to escape their enemies. Movement also brings oxygen into their bodies through deeper breathing and helps circulate oxygen and blood throughout their bodies. It strengthens muscles and generally helps keep animals healthy. Many animals move to play with other animals and/or with people, if they are pets, and to travel from one place to another. We, as human beings, also need to move many times a day

for many of these same reasons. Movement also helps our bodies and minds to work together for learning and more joyful living.

6. Ask for volunteers to tell about some of the ways and different reasons they move throughout their daily activities.

Notes

Activity 22

Moving for Balance

Purpose of this activity: Movement is an effective way to bring the body, mind, and heart into a state of greater balance. It helps to revitalize us and calm us at the same time. The purpose of this activity is to teach children some basic movements to help them feel more balanced, ready to embrace learning more fully, and ready to be with others more joyfully.

Timeframe: about 15 to 30 minutes

What you need: an adequate floor space for movement

What to do:

1. Tell the children they are going to be doing a variety of movements that will help them become more calm and, at the same time, increase their energy. It will also help their bodies, minds, and hearts work better together.

2. Start out by demonstrating movements (see ideas below), then ask the children to join in and do the movements as many times as you like. Be as creative as possible, and encourage the children to get into the movements by playing soft music in the background. Some possibilities include:

    *   Do both horizontal and vertical movements of the arms, legs, and torso.

    *   Use some across-the-midline movements, such as making figure eights in front of you, first with the right arm, then the left arm, then with both arms simultaneously.

    *   Walk in place with arms at your side.

    *   Stretch by reaching your hands as high above your head as possible, while rising up on your toes. As you lower your arms, slowly transfer your weight to your heels.

    *   Wave your arms (like a hula dancer), starting with the right arm extended horizontally about chest level and the left arm at waist level parallel to the right arm. Then, wave to the left, allowing the left arm to rise to the chest level while the right hand descends to the waist level. Continue this alternating arm movement for several seconds.

    *   Walking in place, swing your arms backward and forward without touching the person in front of you.

    *   Place your chin on your chest and slowly move your head and torso toward your toes, while dropping your arms so your hands can touch your toes (or stopping sooner if you need to). Then, allow your torso and head to slowly rise until they are again in an upright position, with your head the last to come up.

- Walk in a circle, placing both hands on top of your head, one on top of the other, then reverse the position of your hands, with the other on top, and walk backwards.

- Repeat any of the above movements at a different tempo.

3. As children become more comfortable in doing the movements, ask for volunteers to take turns being the leader.

4. After 5, 10, or 15 minutes of movement (depending on the age group and time allotted), have the children take a few deep breaths (from the lower abdomen) and find a comfortable place to sit.

5. Ask for volunteers to share what they experienced during the movements and how they felt after doing the movements compared to how they felt before they did them. Encourage as many children as possible to give responses. At the completion of the activity, remind the children to use these and other movements on their own whenever they need to get rebalanced, calm down, and/or get energized. Also remind them of the importance of doing a variety of movements several times a day for health reasons and to help their bodies, minds, and hearts to work more efficiently together.

Notes

Activity 23

Keep an Exercise Journal—and Get Moving!

Purpose of this activity: Children may not give thought to how much exercise they are getting or whether they are getting enough of the right kind. The purpose of this activity is to raise their awareness of the benefits of exercise and track their own levels of exercise so they can adjust, if necessary, to promote their own strength and health.

Timeframe: initially, about 45 minutes for discussion and to make their Exercise Journals, then about 5-10 minutes a day to record in their journals. (Determine how many days or weeks you would like to extend this activity, but aim for a minimum of one week to build awareness.)

What you need: enough white paper for each child to make a journal, with a page for each day that you plan to record in it; writing and drawing utensils (colors); athletic-shoe laces (can be colorful) to tie the pages together in the middle (one per child)

What to do:

1. Start with a discussion of exercise. Ask the children to help you list the benefits of exercise on the board or a flipchart. Draw out from them or add benefits such as:

    *   strengthens our muscles
    *   strengthens our hearts
    *   improves blood flow
    *   strengthens our lungs so we get enough oxygen from the air
    *   sharpens our minds with the extra oxygen and blood flow
    *   burns calories from food for energy
    *   burns extra fat we don't need
    *   lifts our moods
    *   makes us feel better all over

2. Explain to the children that there are basically two kinds of exercise. One mostly strengthens muscles. This kind of exercise usually involves lifting, pushing, pulling, or bending. Lifting any kind of weight is a strengthening exercise. The other kind is called aerobic, which exercises your heart by making it beat faster and your lungs by making them work harder to get air in and out. It also burns more fat, because you're moving faster and using up more calories. Running, swimming, biking, and most other sports are aerobic. Of course, many activities involve both strengthening and aerobic exercise. We need both kinds of exercise to stay strong and healthy.

3. Ask for volunteers to tell what kinds of exercise they get on a regular basis. This can be anything from sports to climbing stairs, walking, or running. It doesn't have to be organized exercise. Get them to think about all their activities during the day. How much time do they just sit and watch television? That doesn't count as exercise!

4. Tell the children they are going to make exercise journals to help them become more aware of the amount and different kinds of exercise they get on a daily basis. They can both write and draw in their journals.

5. Pass out paper for the journals. Tell the children to put the sheets together and fold them in half horizontally so the sheets are in booklet form. (If they have too many sheets to fold at once, they can fold them a few at a time.) Have them tie the pages together by wrapping a shoelace around the crease and tying it in a bow on the outside.

6. Have the children write "Exercise Journal" on the front and decorate the front and back covers with pictures that represent the kinds of exercise they do or represent the benefits of exercise in general.

7. On the inside of the front cover, have them write "Benefits of Exercise" (or "Exercise Helps") at the top of the page and write down the benefits of exercise you've discussed from the list you've posted. They can abbreviate if they want or draw pictures representing the benefits (heart, lungs, brain, muscles…).

8. Tell the children to notice as they go about their days how much and what kind of exercise they get. Each day for a week or month or whatever timeframe you choose, have the children record their exercise through writing or pictures and date the pages.

9. As the time goes on, discuss what they have been doing for exercise. Is it primarily strengthening exercise (what part of the body?), or is it aerobic? Is it both? How much time do the children spend sitting (watching television, for example) compared to the time they are moving about? Do they think they need more exercise? In what ways do they think they can increase their exercise? Brainstorm with them, then follow up at a later date and ask what has changed in the amount of exercise they get and how their bodies responded. Have they noticed a change in their thinking and feeling? Although excess should be avoided, the goal is to get moving—and everything should improve.

Notes

Activity 24

Creating a Positive Learning Experience

Purpose of this activity: Children (and adults) can best utilize all their resources for learning if they feel good about themselves as learners and have clear thinking and relaxed bodies while engaged in the learning process. The purpose of this activity is to help children establish a process to facilitate more effective and enjoyable learning.

Timeframe: about 45 minutes for older children. For younger children, this activity can be adapted to about 15-30 minutes.

What you need: one blank sheet of paper (optional), one Appendix Activity 11, and writing/drawing utensils for each child

What to do:

1. Ahead of time, decide on a short learning task for the children to do that is appropriate for the age group.

2. In preparation for doing the task, lead the children through the following process:

    Have them think of a time when they felt good about what they did or what they learned. To help them connect with this experience, encourage them to visualize that time in their minds. (If they are comfortable doing so, closing their eyes will help them focus and "see" the mental images.) Guide them through the visualization by asking the following questions, leaving a little time between questions for them to access the memories:

    What were you doing at the time? How did you feel about yourself? How did you feel about what you were doing? How did your body feel? Where were you, and what was the space around you like?

    Allow the children two to three minutes to connect with their good experiences.

3. Then, have the children share their memories with the person next to them, or give them the option to briefly sketch pictures of their images on their blank sheets of paper.

4. From what they discovered about these times when they felt successful, help them recreate the positive feelings they had about themselves as learners any time they need to do learning tasks at home or school.

    Start by having them get comfortable and relax their bodies by taking three or four deep breaths from the lower abdominal area, by playing relaxing instrumental music, and/or by having them trace figure eights in front of their chests with one hand at a time then both hands. Point out that we can think more clearly and effectively if our bodies are relaxed.

5. Ask the children to repeat after you the following positive statements about themselves as learners:

I can do this work.
I can think clearly.
I can be successful in doing this task.
I feel good about myself as a learner.
I remember what I am learning.
It's okay to make mistakes while I'm learning. I learn from my mistakes.
Learning gets easier and easier for me as I practice.

Ask for volunteers to suggest other positive statements about learning.

6. Next, explain the task you have decided to have the children do, and tell them how much time they will have to complete it. Ask them to make their own silent statements of confidence about doing the task and to take about two minutes (with eyes closed) to relax by breathing deeply and rhythmically, while mentally picturing themselves successfully completing the task.

7. Give the children the allotted time for the task. You may choose to play relaxing music with 60-70 beats per minute during this period of time. Instrumental music is best for this purpose.*

8. When the time is up or the task is completed, have the children talk about what this process was like for them and whether it helped them feel good about themselves as learners. Feeling good about themselves as learners should free up more inner resources for learning.

9. Pass out the activity sheets from the Appendix that you copied for the children. Review the steps of the process with them, and have them put stars by any of the positive affirmations about learning that helped them. Give them time to write additional affirmations that appeal to them. Remind the children that they can use this same creative learning process when they are doing homework or working independently on learning tasks at school. With practice, the process will become automatic.

* For ideas of relaxing music to play, see *The Mozart Effect* (by Don Campbell) and the music series *Relax with the Classics* (LIND Institute), both listed in the Resources section.

Notes

Activity 25

Five-Minute Mind Teaser

Purpose of this activity: This short activity will encourage children to think outside the box, or approach problems in different ways.

Timeframe: five minutes

What you need: one Appendix Activity 12 for each child

What to do:

1. Pass out the Appendix Activity 12 exercise and read the instructions to the children that are on the sheet:

   Cross out six letters so that the name of a common fruit is left.

   S B I A X L N E A T N T E R A S

2. If after five minutes no one has gotten it, show them the answer (which is given below). Point out that sometimes we have to think in different ways to solve problems.

Answer:

Cross out the letters: S I X L E T T E R S, and you end up with B A N A N A.

Notes

Activity 26

My Amazing Brain

Purpose of this activity: The brain is a complex information system that has three primary functions: thinking, feeling, and survival. The purpose of this activity is to introduce children to these primary functions.

Timeframe: about 15 minutes

What you need: a comfortable space for the children to sit

What to do:

1. Ask the children to be seated comfortably, listen carefully, and follow your hand movements and these instructions:

   - Place your two hands in front of you, with the palms of your hands facing each other as if you were holding a ball.
   - Make a soft fist with each hand.
   - Bring your two fists together so they touch each other, and position them at chest level.
   - Cross your thumbs so the left thumb touches the right fist and the right thumb touches the left fist.
   - Rotate your two fists so you are looking down on your knuckles.

2. As the children are looking down on their knuckles, tell them that this is the approximate size of their brains. With older children, you can tell them that the brain weighs about one pound at birth and about three pounds in adulthood. (If you like, you can bring in objects that weigh one and three pounds as examples.) Allow the children to make any comments at this point.

3. Explain to the children (as they look down on their knuckles) that the thumbs are the front of the brain. For older children, also explain that the thumbs are crossed to remind us that the left side of the brain controls the right side of the body, and the right side of the brain controls the left side of the body. For all children, tell them that the knuckles and outside part of the hands represent the thinking part of the brain, which is called the cerebrum.

4. Have the children spread their palms apart while keeping the knuckles touching. Have them rotate their hands so they can look down at the tips of their fingers. The tips of the fingers represent the part of the brain that houses the emotional or feeling functions of the brain. Have them note that this system is buried deep within the brain and is oftentimes referred to as the limbic or emotional system.

5. Have the children rotate their fists so they are again looking down on their knuckles. Have them draw their forearms together. Tell them to rotate their fists outward so they can see the upper part of their hands and wrists. This area represents the cerebellum and brainstem, which carry out the movement and survival functions of the brain.

6.   Have the children return their hands to a normal position. Ask for volunteers to name the primary functions of the brain. Allow the children to ask any questions they have and/or make any comments about their amazing brains.

Notes

Activity 27

Brainstorming for Balance

Purpose of this activity: Brainstorming results in a variety of options from which to choose. This wider array of possibilities can help bring more balance into our lives. Brainstorming encourages creativity without the threat of being judged for your thoughts. It is also a cooperative process in which the final outcome is greater than any one individual effort. The purpose of this activity is to introduce children to the brainstorming process and the benefits they can derive from engaging in this type of process.

Timeframe: about 15-30 minutes for each part

What you need: flipchart or poster board and markers; Appendix Activity 13 (Guidelines for Brainstorming for your own reference)

What to do:

Part 1

1. Introduce this activity by having the children recall a storm that they were in or have watched. Have them think for a few moments about their experiences relative to the elements of the storm, such as the wind, rain or snow, and how long the storm lasted.

2. Next, have the children share their observations about the wind, precipitation, and length of the storm. Then, point out that in sharing their ideas about what they observed, there were no right or wrong ideas and there were many differences in what they saw and experienced. Also point out that storms take their own course—i.e., no one controls them.

3. Ask the children how many of them have heard the word brainstorming. Ask for volunteers to share their ideas of what brainstorming means. Emphasize the fact that brainstorming is allowing as many thoughts as possible to flow from your brain without interruption, questions, or comments. Just as storms take their course, thoughts come and are expressed without trying to control them. There are no right or wrong ideas. When everyone has run out of ideas, the brainstorming process stops.

4. Begin the brainstorming process by providing a stimulus appropriate for the age of the children who are participating. The stimulus can be either a problem-solving question to obtain as many solutions as possible for a current situation or problem or a creative stimulus to activate the creativity and imagination of the children. For example:

    Problem-solving stimulus: What can we do to make our playground more safe and fun?

    Creative stimulus: Here are three balls of different sizes and colors. Come up with as many things as possible that we can do with these balls.

    As you begin the brainstorming process with the children, remind them of the following guidelines. (Also refer to the Guidelines for Brainstorming in Appendix Activity 13.)

- There are no right or wrong answers.
- Only one person speaks at a time while the others listen.
- No questions or comments can be made when an answer is given.
- Each child can contribute any number of ideas.
- You can pass if you don't have an idea when it comes to your turn.
- The brainstorming process stops when no one can offer any more ideas.

5. Record the ideas as the children give them. For older children, you may choose one of the children to do the recording. When the brainstorming process is completed, count the number of ideas generated and point out how this cooperative effort came up with many more ideas than one person could. This gives us many more options and helps us to expand on our own ideas. It also gives us a wider range of ideas, thus creating the possibility of making balanced choices.

Part 2

1. For older children, vary the approach to brainstorming by having them write their responses rather than giving them orally. With the written approach, divide the children into groups of four or five. Provide each group with the same stimulus, a sheet of paper, and writing utensils.

2. Have one child in each group write his or her response at the top of the paper then pass the paper to the next child until each child has had a turn. Keep repeating this process until all ideas have been given. Anyone who doesn't have an idea to write down should be given the option to pass.

3. When all groups have finished, have one group at a time share their responses with the rest of the children.

4. Ask the children what they learned from doing this form of brainstorming and how they might use this idea in other situations.

Notes

Activity 28

Mind Mapping:
A Balanced Way to Organize Ideas

Purpose of this activity: When we use both sides of our brains (our "whole" brains—both the analytical and intuitive/creative aspects), we are more effective and efficient in organizing, recalling, utilizing, and communicating information. The purpose of this activity is to teach children the process of mind mapping, a way to organize information by using both sides of the brain to bring about a greater degree of balance.

You might want to do Activity 27 on brainstorming before this activity, as mind mapping is a more structured and graphic form of brainstorming.

Timeframe: about 30-45 minutes

What you need: flipchart, drawing paper, black and various colors of markers, colored pencils, or crayons; Appendix Activity 14 examples of mind mapping and instructions (which you may copy for the children or just use as references for yourself)

What to do:

1.   Introduce this activity by presenting the following information about mind mapping in whatever way is appropriate for the age group:

     "You can organize your thoughts in different ways. You can make a map of your thoughts that will help you use more of your brains and make organizing your ideas and thoughts easier and more fun. You can use mind mapping when you want to organize your thoughts for giving a talk or writing about a topic. It helps you know where to start and what to cover. The process is something like brainstorming, but you use different colors to draw a map as you go and put similar ideas together on your map."

2.   Show the children how to make a mind map by drawing one on your flipchart with their input. You'll find examples in Appendix Activity 14 (both using an object as the main topic for younger children and using a concept as the main topic for older children). If you like, you can use one of these topics, or pick your own. The steps of building a mind map are below and also in Appendix Activity 14.

     A.   Use black to draw all lines and ovals and to write linking words, and use colors to write the words in the ovals. Start by writing the main topic word in one color in an oval in the middle of your page.

     B.   Draw a line out from the main topic and write a linking word across or by the line. (For object topics, start with linking words such as *is, are,* or *have.*)

C. Brainstorm ideas that can follow from that linking word. Write them all in a different color from the main topic word. Make all the words stemming from one main link the same color.

D. Using black again, draw lines out from these new topics using linking words.

E. Brainstorm ideas that come from the new topics.

F. Try different linking words from the main topic and see what you can brainstorm. (For example, if your first linking word was *are,* try the linking word *have.)*

G. Keep drawing links until you can't think of any more ideas.

3. When you and the children have completed the sample mind map (which may differ from the example in the Appendix, if you have asked for their input), give them all sheets of paper and drawing utensils, and have them create their own mind maps with topics of their choice. If you feel they aren't ready to do this on their own yet, have them help you create another mind map on the flipchart.

4. If you like, you may give all the children copies of either or both mind-map examples from the Appendix for future reference.

5. When time allows, and if you think the children are ready for it, assign them short speeches or essays for which they can choose the topic, and have them begin the assignment by mind mapping it.

Notes

Activity 29

Step-by-Step Problem Solving

Purpose of this activity: When faced with a problem, it's advantageous to have a process for solving it. This activity gives children a step-by-step way to tackle problems, which helps prevent a confused, shotgun approach or freezing up and not getting anywhere. The process can be used with a single child or a group. Once the children have been guided through it a few times, they should be able to do it on their own.

Timeframe: about 30 minutes

What you need: chalkboard, whiteboard, flipchart, or poster board and appropriate writing utensils

What to do:

1. Explain to the children that you're going to give them a way to help solve problems and that you'll help them with it until they can do it on their own.

2. Go over the following steps to problem solving with the children. A short version follows, which you can write on the board, a flipchart, or poster to help them remember as you explain it and to use for future reference. (A poster would be best for future reference, although you could write it first on the board and later render it more artistically on a poster. Perhaps the children could do this and illustrate the poster.)

   A. Explain the problem, describing it as clearly as you can. Maybe draw a picture of it.

   B. Say how you feel about the problem. (If you are doing this alone, just tune in to your feelings so you know what they are.)

   C. Use the Tapping Game on the problem. (See Tapping Game Guide, Appendix Activity 16, for how to use tapping on a problem. This is optional, but it helps release negative feelings around the problem so it's easier to resolve the problem in a clearer and more rational state of mind.)

   D. Choose how you want to feel.

   E. Decide what outcome you would like to have. Make sure it will not hurt or be bad for anyone else and, ideally, will be good for everyone involved. (Realize that this is what you would prefer but that it may not work out exactly that way. Be willing to be flexible. Maybe you'll end up with something even better.)

   F. Brainstorm possible ways to solve the problem. (Brainstorming is listing every idea that comes into your mind without judging it. If the whole class is brainstorming, no one is allowed to judge another's ideas, either.)

   G. Choose an action to take that came up in brainstorming.

   H. Take it!

I.   If it worked, celebrate!

J.   If it didn't, try another way.

K.   Don't give up until something works. If necessary, ask a grownup for help.

Here is a short version of the steps for a poster, after you have explained them:

A.   Explain the problem.
B.   Say how you feel.
C.   Do the Tapping Game on the problem.
D.   Choose how you want to feel.
E.   Decide best outcome.
F.   Brainstorm solutions.
G.   Choose an action.
H.   Take it!
I.   If it worked—yay!
J.   If it didn't, try another way.
K.   Don't give up!

3.   Help the children role play problem solving. They may use either problems they currently have or hypothetical problems.

4.   Whenever a problem arises in class, take the opportunity to go through the steps of problem solving with the children.

5.   Don't give up! ☺

Notes

Activity 30

The Energy of Words

Purpose of this activity: Everything within and around us consists of energy. This energy affects us in positive or negative ways, or it may have a neutral effect on us. Words, as energy, have the power to affect our feelings about ourselves, our moods, and the physiology of our bodies, such as heart rate variability, pulse rate, blood pressure, and energy level. The purpose of this activity is to help children become more aware of how words affect them.

Timeframe: 30-45 minutes

What you need: a flipchart or poster board, writing utensils, one 3-x-5-inch note card for each child

What to do:

1. Introduce this activity by sharing the following information with the children using wording your age group can understand.

    Dr. Masaru Emoto, a Japanese scientist, has done many experiments with water. In his work taking photographs of frozen water crystals, he discovered that words, emotions, and even music have great effects on water. When he exposed water to positive verbal or written words such as *Thank you, Love,* and *Gratitude,* he found that the water formed beautiful and complete crystals. When water was exposed to words that create emotional stress, such as *You fool* and *You make me sick,* the photographs of the frozen water showed ugly formless masses. Since our bodies are three-fourths water (about 70 percent) or more, these scientific experiments show us that we need to think about how our words and the words of others affect our minds and our bodies.

    If you have Dr. Emoto's book available (see Resources), this would be a good time to show the children his magnified photographs of water under different conditions.

2. Ask the children to think about some feeling words or phrases that they hear every day. These could be words they have said to others, that others have said to them, or that they have heard in conversations or through the media. List these words on the flipchart as the children come up with them. When all the children's words have been recorded, have the children look at the first word or phrase in the list. As you say it to them, have them sense if the word makes them have a positive feeling, no particular feeling (neutral), or a negative feeling. Depending on the children's responses, place a *P* in front of the word or phrase if it has a positive effect, an *0* if it has a neutral effect, and an *N* if it has a negative effect on them. For younger children, you may want to substitute good (+) and bad (-) for positive and negative. Continue in the same manner until you have finished the list of words.

3. Go through the list a second time, but focus only on the positive words by having the children say each positive word in unison, pausing to sense how the word feels, and then continuing until you are through the list.

4. Have the children reflect on how they felt as each positive word or phrase was said. Then have them choose the positive word/s that had the warmest, most supportive, or encouraging effect on them. Have them write this word or phrase or draw a picture to represent it on a 3-x-5-inch card.

5. Placing their cards in front of themselves, have the children say the words or phrases aloud to themselves five times.

6. Encourage the children to remember their words or phrases, so that any time someone says an unkind or put-down word or a word that makes them feel not very good, they can say their words to themselves in order to counteract any negative effect unkind or put-down words have had.

7. Suggest the children take their cards home and put them where they are visible, so whenever they need a positive emotional charge, they can say their chosen words to themselves.

8. See Activity 31 for an informal experiment mentioned in Dr. Emoto's book that the children can conduct to see if positive and negative words can physically affect cooked rice.

Notes

Activity 31

Mind and Matter: An Experiment

Purpose of this activity: This experiment clearly demonstrates the power of words, thoughts, and intentions. It will make the children more aware of how they affect the world around them and should encourage them to adjust their words, thoughts, and intentions to be more positive. The experiment is based on one mentioned in the book *Messages from Water* by Masaru Emoto (see Resources).

Timeframe: just a few minutes a day over two weeks, with an initial introduction of 10 minutes

What you need: two glass jars with lids, each holding one cup of cooked rice. (If you have small jars, you can use less rice.)

What to do:

1. You will have to cook the rice ahead of time and put it in the two jars.

2. As an introduction, you might want to get a copy of the book *Messages from Water*. Show the children the pictures of the highly magnified frozen water that came from jars that had the words *Thank you* and *You make me sick. I will kill you.* taped on them. The first one shows a beautiful, light-colored crystal, and the second one shows a darker, shapeless, unpleasant-looking mass.

    Tell the children they will be doing an experiment to determine if their intentions and words have an effect on cooked rice, as you don't have the equipment to do the magnified frozen water experiments. Show them the two jars of rice.

3. On one jar, tape a piece of paper that has *Thank you!* written on it. On the other jar, tape a piece of paper that has *You dummy!* written on it. Place the jars in two different corners of the room. Tell the children that every day when they come in (or pick a time), they are to go to each jar of rice in turn and do the following:

    *   Say "Thank you!" to the jar of rice that has *Thank you!* taped on it.
    *   Say "You dummy!" to the jar of rice that has *You dummy!* taped on it.

    They do not need to say these things loudly, but they should say them as if they mean them. If necessary, remind the children to do this throughout the experiment (and try not to feel sorry for the "dummy" rice!). If you like, you can do this experiment with just the taped words.

4. Watch what happens to each jar of rice over two weeks. Discuss the results with the children. What are the implications of these results in our daily lives?

Notes

Activity 32

Words Can Be Our Friends

Purpose of this activity: Words have power, and we should use them responsibly. The purpose of this activity is to help the children understand how our words affect us and to encourage them to speak in ways that are more beneficial to their well-being.

Timeframe: Part 1—about 30 minutes; Part 2—about 30 minutes. (You may choose to do these activities on separate days.)

What you need: chalkboard and chalk (different colors, if you like) and a basket full of small squares or rectangles of paper with "dump truck" and "balloon" words written on them (optional—see below)

What to do:

Part 1: Dump Truck and Balloon Words

1. On the board, draw a giant hot-air balloon with a basket under it. If you have colored chalk, make it colorful! Draw a rainbow above it, if you like. Beside it, draw a big dump truck. It can have its bed tipped, as if it's dumping a load. Use brown or gray or just plain white chalk. You may want to draw these before the class starts.

2. Let the children know that today's discussion is about words and how they make us feel. Ask them to take a few minutes to think of words that either make them feel down in the dumps or lift them up. Tell them to raise their hands when they have a word in mind. Explain that when you point to someone, that person is to say his or her word, and the rest of the class is to call out either "dump truck" or "balloon," depending on whether the word makes them feel down in the dumps or it lifts them up. Give the children an example, such as the word *friend*. Ask if it is a dump truck or balloon word. Provide another word, such as *angry*. Dump truck or balloon? Write each word on its appropriate graphic. The balloon words could be in the basket of the balloon or on the balloon. You might want to have the dump truck words spilling out the back of the dump truck's bed.

    If you think the children will not be able to come up with enough words or the right kind of words, you could have a basket of words on pieces of paper that they could take turns drawing and reading. Dump truck words might be words such as *no, impossible, wrong, bad, war, hate, ugly, sick, fear, pain, trouble, sad, can't, don't, icky, boring, dull, nasty, never.* Balloon words might be words such as *yes, good, peace, love, thanks, happy, kind, smile, warm, fuzzy, cute, beautiful, laugh, like, exciting, great, terrific, pleased, know, wise, sure, successful, can, joy.*

3. Write the words that the children give you on the dump truck or the balloon, depending on where the children say they should go. When they can think of no more words that fit the categories or have read all the words in the basket, ask them to read each group of words all together to see how the words make them feel. Tell them to think about the meaning of the words as they say them. Start with the dump truck words, then ask the children how they are feeling. Follow with the balloon words, then ask if those words create a different feeling.

4. Wrap up Part 1 by asking the children what they learned and how they will think differently about the words they use.

Part 2: Dump Truck and Balloon Stories

1. Tell the children you'd like them to write a story using dump truck words and then write one using balloon words.

2. If the children are old enough, they can write their own stories. Otherwise, help them compose one jointly:

    Ask someone to suggest a main character. Ask someone else to give a location where the action will take place. Have each child contribute a sentence using one of the dump truck words. (Or, call on just a few children to save time and limit the length of your story, if need be.) When you have completed your downer of a story, read it through and ask the children how it makes them feel.

    Using the same procedure, have the children compose a story using balloon words. Read the completed story and ask the children how it makes them feel.

3. Alternatively, you might have the children fill in the blanks of a story in which you have already supplied the dump truck words. For example:

    Joey hated _____. He thought he would never be able to _____. He was wrong when he _____ and bad when he _____. It was an icky day when he found out that _____. "It's so much trouble to _____," said Joey. "I can't even _____. I'm afraid to _____, and I'm sick of _____."

    Using balloon words, the story might be something like this:

    "I know I can _____," said Dave. He laughed as he thought about _____. He was happy that _____. What a great _____! He felt pleased that _____. He could see in his mind that _____ would be successful.

    When your stories are complete, read them through and ask the children how the stories make them feel. Do they feel dumped or lifted up?

4. Talk with the children about how they use words in their lives. Remind them that thoughts are really words that we don't say out loud—and spoken words are really thoughts that we do say out loud. Whether we think them or say them, our words can put us in the dumps or lift us up.

5. Ask the children to be aware of whether they usually think and talk like dump trucks or balloons. Make sure they realize that everyone has dump truck times or dump truck days. Likewise, some days we are lifted as high as rainbows or float happily along with the clouds. Tell the children that it helps us feel happier to think and say more balloon words than dump truck words. Ask them:

    Do you say Yes more than No?

    Do you say or think words such as …
        I can do it.
        I'll figure this out.
        I can find a way.

I'm good at this.
I like myself.

Or do you more often say or think …
I can't do it.
I'll never figure this out.
I did something wrong, so I'm a bad person.
I'm not as good as everyone else.
I'm stupid.

6.   Talk about how feelings sometimes come up that can make us want to say and think dump truck words—because feelings affect our words, just as words affect our feelings. It's okay, and even good, to say, "I'm sad," when you're sad or "I'm angry," when you're angry. The problem comes when we are continually saying words that are downers, because we pull ourselves down. The idea is to start becoming aware of the words we use on a regular basis. Balloon words can help us stay out of the dumps.

Notes

Activity 33

Creating Sculpture Collages

Purpose of this activity: This activity exercises creativity. It helps to develop the right brain, because it is spatial and intuitive rather than linear and analytical like the left brain. To be a balanced individual, both types of activities are necessary.

Timeframe: 45 minutes to one hour

What you need: many types of objects, which can be either natural, man-made, or both. It helps if these materials are fairly small and lightweight, as they will be affixed together in a sculpture. You will also need strong, fast-drying glue or two-sided sticky pads used to hang things on walls, or string or wire to combine the materials. Slips of paper and writing utensils will be needed to label the sculptures.

What to do:

1. Explain to the children that they will be making sculpture collages. Discuss what a sculpture is and what a collage is. In essence, they will be creating three-dimensional works of art using a variety of materials. They can create something specific (e.g., a dog out of different sizes of pine cones) or something abstract (e.g., a combination of objects that has an interesting or beautiful design or shape or display of colors but is not meant to be anything specific).

2. Make the materials available to the children, perhaps on a large table. Have each child choose objects with which to make a sculpture. (You may want to have them draw numbers for choosing objects to keep it orderly, as they can't all do this at once if it's a large group. Other options are to provide everyone with the same types of objects and see how the children combine them differently, or have the children bring items from home.) Provide the children with whatever you are using to hold the objects together.

3. Tell them to take time to think about what they want to do with their materials. Suggest that they visualize their sculptures in their minds before they actually build them. When they are finished, have them title their sculptures.

4. Have each child tell the group about his or her sculpture. Is it something specific or is it abstract? Why did the child decide to choose those particular objects? How did he or she decide to put them together this way?

5. Have the children write their names on slips of paper along with the titles of their sculptures. Find a place to display the sculptures with the corresponding names and titles.

Notes

Activity 34

Making Friends with a Brush

Purpose of this activity: Engaging in a creative activity helps to quiet the thinking mind and activate the intuitive, imaginative, and creative processes to a greater degree. A person's state of balance is dependent upon using these processes as well as the thinking process. The purpose of this activity is to give children an opportunity to engage in a creative process so they can experience a greater sense of balance and wholeness.

Timeframe: about 30-45 minutes

What you need: watercolor brushes of various sizes, watercolor paints in the primary colors, sheets of watercolor paper, containers for water, containers for mixing colors, paper towels, a tape or CD player, and a tape or CD of soft music

What to do:

1. Introduce this activity to the children by explaining that one of the first things a student of Japanese brush painting is asked to do is to "make friends" with his or her brush/es. (You might show the children an example of Japanese brush painting.) Tell the children that for their art activity today, they also will make friends with their brushes. First they will observe, hold, and touch their brushes, then they will explore the types of strokes the brushes can make using water, and finally, they will explore mixing and using color to create symbols, designs, or pictures with their brushes. Explain that Japanese and Chinese brush painters use special colored inks, brushes, and paper, but that today the children will be using watercolor paints, brushes, and paper, because they are more available and less costly than Japanese or Chinese art materials.

2. Have the children sit comfortably at tables (or other appropriate arrangements), and then ask one person from each table to get a brush, a set of primary colors, and three sheets of watercolor paper for each person at his or her table. Have paper towels on the tables, and tell each child to take a couple of sheets.

3. When everyone has their materials, ask the children to just observe their brushes without picking them up. Have the children do this for about 30 seconds, then stop. Ask volunteers to give their thoughts and observations. Then have them pick up their brushes. Give them 30 seconds to touch the bristles of their brushes and note the softness and flexibility of the bristles. Again give the children a few moments to share their thoughts and observations.

4. Next, have the children dip their brushes in water and make brushstrokes on a piece of paper (first letting the excess water drip off or lightly wiping the brush on the paper towel). Have them compare how working with a brush is different from working with markers, crayons, and pencils—i.e., a brush has more flexibility and requires a softer touch to make the strokes flow freely.

5. Tell the children they are now going to make brushstrokes using color rather than water. Depending on the age group and time available, give them the choice of picking one color or experimenting by mixing two or more primary colors in a small container. (Make sure they understand to rinse the brush between colors and not to use too much water, as then they will have puddles on their papers

and their paintings won't dry fast enough. They can use the paper towels to blot their brushes and wipe them between colors.) Have them make brushstrokes of different lengths and widths going in different directions and creating a variety of effects. Allow them about 3-5 minutes to do this.

6. Now that the children have become more familiar with their brushes and the possible range of color (if they used more than one color in #5), have them use their imaginations to create symbols, designs, or pictures on clean sheets of paper. Suggest they try the Japanese way of painting with a few simple, graceful lines. (Again, you might show examples.) To help children engage in this process more intuitively and creatively, have them close their eyes for a moment and imagine their hands and brushes creating objects or pictures on their papers. Play soft music in the background to facilitate this process. Then have the children open their eyes and put their ideas on paper, leaving the music on while they are painting.

7. After about 5-10 minutes (depending upon the age group), turn off the music and ask the children to rinse off their brushes in their water containers, wipe them dry with the paper towels, and get the paint containers ready for storage. Have one child from each table return the materials back to a central place. (Brushes may need to be more thoroughly cleaned before putting them away.)

8. Have the children remain in their places with their works of art. Ask for volunteers to either share something about their pictures or talk about what the experience of making friends with a brush was like for them. When the sharing is finished, point out that engaging in art is a good idea when they need to quiet their thinking minds and activate their creative processes. We need to balance one with the other. If you have older children, you can encourage them to further explore Sumi-e (Japanese brush painting) or Chinese ink painting. You could have books on the subjects available, or they can check the library.

Notes

Activity 35

What I Like About Myself

Purpose of this activity: It is important that children like themselves if they are to grow up as psychologically and emotionally stable adults. In this activity, they focus on and nurture the good in themselves. It is a short activity that can be done often. It is a good activity to do when children are restless to help them calm down.

Timeframe: five minutes (or about 10-15 if you choose to have the children write)

What you need: no materials needed (optional: writing utensils and Peace Journals—see Activity 50 for making personal Peace Journals)

What to do:

1. Have the children stop what they are doing and either close their eyes or focus on a spot on the floor or their desks in front of them.

2. Ask each to place one hand over his or her heart (demonstrate).

3. Ask the children to think of as many things as they can that they like about themselves. These things don't have to be great or wonderful. They can be based on what the children have done, what they like to do, what they're good at, their qualities, their interests, or whatever. Someone might like his big toe. Someone else might like herself because she fed the dog this morning or is a good friend. Give the children a minute or two to think.

4. An option is to have them write down their thoughts in their Peace Journals (Activity 50), if you would like to make those first.

5. Tell them to carry that warm, fuzzy feeling about themselves throughout the day.

Notes

Activity 36

How Feelings Affect Us

Purpose of this activity: Each day we all have many different feelings. Our thoughts and actions are affected by the feelings we have. The purpose of this activity is to become more aware of our feelings and how they affect us and to learn how to think and act in helpful ways when affected by unhelpful feelings.

Timeframe: about one hour but could be split up if an hour is not available

What you need: pencils, markers or crayons; 8½ -by-11-inch paper—with lines if you have the children write and without lines if you have them draw (see below); a chalkboard, flipchart, or poster board; and one copy for each child of Appendix Activity 15, My Feelings Are Important

What to do:

1. Have each child respond to the incomplete sentences listed below. Adapt how you present the sentences and how to have the children respond to accommodate the age of the children involved. For example, pictures and verbal responses are an appropriate medium for younger children. Have older children write the first part of each sentence then complete it.

    I feel happy when ………
    I feel sad when ………
    I feel squirmy or restless when ………
    I feel calm and peaceful when ………
    I feel angry when ………

    Note: Add any other feeling words that are appropriate for your age group.

2. Discuss how feeling happy affects your thoughts and actions compared to how feeling sad effects your thoughts and actions. Do the same for each of the feelings you include in the incomplete sentence list.

3. Have the children come up with other feelings, such as loving, scared, excited, surprised, worried, embarrassed, etc.

4. Explain to the children that it is natural to have all kinds of feelings. Feelings just come up as we go about our daily lives. Some feel good and others don't. Some are helpful and others aren't. From the list of feelings you and the children have completed, create two other lists. For the first list, identify those feelings that help them have positive and peaceful thoughts and help them have confidence in themselves, in being with others, learning new ideas, and taking actions that are fun and meaningful. You can choose to do this as a group, or have each child complete the first page of the "My Feelings Are Important" Chart. For the second list, identify the feelings that interfere with having positive and peaceful thoughts and for taking positive actions. Again, you can either do this as a group or use the second page of the chart to have children record these feelings.

5. Explain that emotions, thoughts, and actions are all tied together and affect each other. Talk about ways the children can keep the unhelpful feelings from being problems in their lives. Some possible solutions include:

- Notice when you have an unhelpful feeling. Let it be okay that you're having the feeling. Send the feeling love and understanding. It doesn't know that it's unhelpful. Send yourself love and understanding, as it wasn't your fault that you had an unhelpful feeling. It just happened.

- Choose to do something helpful about your unhelpful feeling to turn it around, such as talking about it to a friend or adult that you trust. Say how you feel without blaming anyone about it. Sometimes talking it over helps change the unhelpful feeling into a helpful understanding.

- Do the Tapping Game (Activity 39) with your feeling. See if you can get your feeling down to zero.

6. Ask the children how they can use what they learned about feelings by doing this activity. Then suggest that each child draw a picture and/or write a statement giving one way to use this information in his or her daily life. Predetermine a time to check back with the children to see if and how what they learned is making a difference in what they think about feelings, how they feel about themselves, how they share feelings with others, and what actions they are taking when they get unhelpful feelings.

"There can be no knowledge without emotion. We may be aware of a truth, yet until we have felt its force, it is not ours. To the cognition of the brain must be added the experience of the soul."

Arnold Bennett (1867-1931)

Notes

Activity 37

Sharing, Talking About, and Dealing with Feelings

Purpose of this activity: This activity helps children recognize, name, share, and deal with feelings so they can better understand themselves and have more empathy for others, as well. The different facets of the activity will help children realize they are not alone in feeling their emotions and help them transform or release negative emotions. See Activity 36, How Feelings Affect Us, for another approach to this subject.

Timeframe: This activity has several parts. You may present the parts together or divide them up, as time allows. Approximate timeframes for each part are: Part 1—a half hour; Parts 2, 3, and 4—15 minutes to a half hour each, depending on the size of your group.

What you need: a talking stick (Activity 52); a chalkboard, flipchart, or whiteboard; writing and drawing utensils

What to do:

Part 1: List Feelings

1. Have the children sit on the floor in a circle. Explain that they are all going to create a story together. The story is going to be about a boy and girl who have many adventures and experience many different feelings. Before they start the story, tell them you would like them to come up with a list of feelings that they can use in their story. Ask them to name different feelings, or emotions, so you can write them down.

2. List the feelings the children tell you on the chalkboard, flipchart, or whiteboard. When they have exhausted their ideas, you might want to add some of your own, making sure they understand the meanings of the feelings you add.

3. Ask for volunteers to illustrate the feelings, with a face next to each feeling.

Part 2: Create a Story

1. Tell the children that you will start the story, and then each person will have the opportunity to add a part to the story in which one of the characters experiences one of the feelings you've listed. The story must be related to the previous person's part of the story. Example: You start with, "One day, a boy named Andy and a girl named Christy went to the zoo. They were excited!" The next person picks up the story and says, "They wanted to see the dolphin show but just missed it. They were sad." Then the next person says, "But Andy saw the monkeys playing, and that made him laugh and feel happy again." "Then Christy dropped her ice cream cone and was embarrassed." And so on. Tell the children that they may repeat a feeling, but that eventually you'd like all of the feelings listed to be used in the story.

2. Introduce the idea of using the talking stick (if they haven't previously made talking sticks and you haven't at that time explained how to use them). Tell the children that only the one holding the talking stick can speak, and everyone else must listen to that person without interrupting. When the child with the talking stick is finished with his part of the story, he hands the stick to the next person in the circle to add another part. Encourage everyone to participate, but if someone is not able to think of anything to say, he or she may keep the talking stick moving to the next person. The last child will hand the stick back to you, and you will finish the story with some kind of "happy ending."

Part 3: Sharing Your Own Emotions

1. When the story is over, ask for volunteers to share times when they have felt the feelings the characters in the story felt. Put the talking stick in the center of the circle and tell the children to pick up the stick when they are ready to share and put it back when they are finished.

2. When everyone has had an opportunity to share, talk about ways to change uncomfortable feelings into positive, or at least neutral, feelings. Using the talking stick, ask the children to share ideas. You may sit in the circle also, so you can add ideas when they run out. Possible ideas are:

   - Talk your feelings out with a friend or adult you trust.
   - Don't make the feeling bad or yourself bad for feeling it. It is just a feeling, and you couldn't help feeling it at the time. It's okay.
   - Allow yourself to feel the feeling fully, then change your focus to something more pleasant.
   - Do the Tapping Game with the feeling. (See Activity 39 and Part 4 below.)
   - Place both hands on your heart, close your eyes, and picture someone or some place you love or a pet you love.

Part 4: Using the Tapping Game for Feelings

See suggestions for using the Tapping Game for feelings in the Tapping Game Guide, Appendix Activity 16. Explain this purpose for the tapping, and practice the procedure with the children.

Notes

Activity 38

Recognizing and Changing Feelings

Purpose of this activity: When we become more aware of our feelings, we can choose which ones we wish to embrace and which ones we want to neutralize or exchange for a feeling that affects us in a positive way. The purpose of this activity is to encourage children to notice how their feelings affect them and then make a conscious decision to focus on good feelings and those that help them perform well. By the same process, they can consciously choose to neutralize or replace a negative feeling with a positive one.

Timeframe: about 15-30 minutes

What you need: 3-x-5-inch cards and pencils and markers; a list of feeling words or series of pictures that depict feelings

What to do:

1. Greet the children as they come in the door. Hand each one a card and a pencil. Have them pause for a moment after they sit down and connect with how they are feeling. Ask them each to write a word or phrase or draw a picture or symbol to describe how they are feeling in that moment. Then, have them rate themselves from 1 (if they are feeling very sad, angry, discouraged…) to 5 (if they are feeling great, upbeat, very positive, happy…) and write their number ratings on their cards.

2. After all the children have entered the room, have them join you in a circle and ask for volunteers to share how they rated their feelings.

3. From the list of feeling words or pictures, have each child choose a word or two or a picture that best describes the feeling that was the basis for his or her rating. Have the children write or draw these choices on their cards.

4. If the words or pictures describe ratings of 1 or 2, have them use a red marker to underline their responses, if a 3, underline with yellow, and if a 4 or 5, underline with green. Explain that green means go with the feeling, yellow means you may want to move into a more positive feeling, and red means you want to stop and neutralize that feeling or move it into the green zone if you can.

5. Ask the children who have green-zone ratings to voluntarily share with the rest of the children the words or pictures they used from the master list to describe their ratings of 4 or 5. Then, encourage the children who rated themselves in the yellow or red zone to choose words or pictures that have the potential to help them feel more positive, which, in turn, will help them perform more effectively on the tasks they will be doing today.

6. After the children with ratings in the yellow and red zones have chosen new words or pictures, have them put big Xs through their first ratings and turn their cards over to now rate themselves on how they would like to feel. Then, have them write the word/s or draw the pictures to support this rating. Remind all the children that what we focus on influences how we feel and what happens to us.

7. After some time has passed and just before the children leave the room, have everyone rate themselves again. Have them note any differences between their first and second ratings (before and after focusing on having positive feelings). If this process has been successful for them, remind them that they can use this technique whenever they need to refocus their feelings. If some children were not successful with this process, set a time aside in the near future when you can work with these children further.

Note: This activity can be used as often as needed and can be adapted to fit into a five-minute time slot.

"If you are distressed by anything external, the pain is not due to the thing itself, but to your estimate of it; and this you have the power to revoke at any moment."

Marcus Aurelius

Notes

Activity 39

The Tapping Game

Purpose of this activity: The body includes a system of energy pathways. Sometimes these pathways become blocked, creating emotional and physical distress. This activity provides a simple way of releasing the blocked energy, which, in turn, releases the emotional and/or physical distress, depending on its complexity.

The main purpose here is to help children release any anxiety, stress, or just plain restlessness that interferes with effective learning. Thus, although this technique is physical and used on the physical body, it demonstrates how the body, mind, and emotions are closely interconnected.

The tapping technique, which you will introduce as a game in this activity, is a useful tool for children (or anyone) to help themselves calm down, release stress, and sometimes release physical pain or discomfort, depending on its cause. It can be introduced to children as a way of helping themselves feel happier and more peaceful when something is bothering them or they just feel restless and need to calm down and focus on a task. As a teacher or parent, you will benefit from the children using this technique and also can benefit from using it yourself in stressful situations.

Timeframe: initially about 30 minutes, but once the children learn the technique, it can be done in as little as five minutes

What you need: one copy per child of the appropriate page (for the age group) in the Appendix Activity 16 Tapping Game Guide that shows where to tap. The other pages in the Guide are for your reference so you can guide the children in the tapping.

What to do:

1. First, learn the tapping technique yourself, using the Activity 16 Tapping Game Guide in the Appendix. Practice on yourself in situations where you have physical or emotional distress, and notice how it works. You might try it on that occasional headache or when your day isn't going very well and you're stressed out. See if you can bring your distress to 0, wherever you start on the scale of 0 to 10 (where 10 is extreme distress and 0 is total relief from distress).

2. Try introducing the Tapping Game on a day when the children are restless and need calming down. (To yourself, rate their restlessness as a whole on a scale of 0 to 10, with 0 being very calm and 10 being wild. That way you can clearly judge the results after they've tapped.)

   When you are ready to introduce it, tell the children you are going to show them the Tapping Game. Depending on the age of the group, you can explain that they can use the Tapping Game to:

   IMPROVE PERFORMANCE in a sport or other activity. (This should get their attention.)

   CALM DOWN whenever they are upset or restless or need to release any negative emotions.

   FOCUS on a task to help them do their best.

IMPROVE TEST SCORES. (In fact, it would be helpful to lead the whole group through the procedure right before each test you give. The tapping relieves nervousness and thus is especially valuable for those with pronounced test anxiety, but it can help anyone's mental focus.)

SOMETIMES HELP RELIEVE PAIN when they're hurting physically. (This works if there is an emotional component to the pain, which often there is, even if we aren't aware of it, so it's worth a try.)

More ideas are listed in the Appendix Tapping Game Guide.

3. Tell the children that today you're going to play the Tapping Game to help them calm down so they can learn better. Then, lead them through the steps of the game. (You can have them follow you first, and later pass out the sheet with the graphic showing the spots to tap for future reference and to reinforce what you've done.)

Ask them to decide how restless they are on a scale of 0–10, where 0 is perfectly calm and 10 is really, really restless. If they are just a little restless, they might be at a 4. If they are quite restless but not horribly restless, they might be at a 7 or 8.

You could draw this continuum on the board or a sheet of paper to show it graphically. Also, it may help to hold your hands out in front of you and show them that hands held far apart represent 10 (VERY restless) and hands together (as if you were in a prayer position) represent 0 (perfectly calm).

Each child needs to determine his or her own state of restlessness, as the children will vary. Help the younger children decide how restless they are. If someone can't come up with a number, have the child show you using the hand method and assign a number based on how far apart the hands are.

Tell everyone that the goal of the game is to get yourself down to 0. Let them know that it doesn't matter where they start. It's possible to go from 10 to 0 just as fast as it is to go from 4 or 5 to 0. They just need to be honest about where they are on the scale.

Tapping the "karate chop" spot on the hand gently but firmly, say three times: "Even though I'm antsy (or restless) right now and can't sit still, I'm really a good kid." (This is the "kickoff.")

Go through the tapping spots, tapping about 5-10 times on each spot and using the focus phrase "this antsy (or restless) feeling."

After one round, ask the children to reassess where they are on the scale of 0-10. Did their restlessness go down? Are they feeling completely calm yet? Ask for volunteers to tell the group their previous scores and their scores now from self-assessment. (Or use the hand scale.)

If they aren't all at 0, do another round of the Tapping Game. Everyone can do it again just for practice, even if some are at 0. Tell the 0 group they are supporting the others in bringing their scores down to 0. This time, say: "Even though I'm still restless, I like myself anyway (or I'm still a good kid)." The focus phrase this time is "rest of this antsiness" (or "remaining restlessness").

Have everyone check their bodies again to see if they are totally calm (0). This, in itself, is a good exercise for body awareness. If they aren't all at 0 yet, you can decide if they are calm enough for now or if you want to do another round and bring their scores down further.

When you finish, congratulate everyone for their good jobs playing the game. Tell them you'll be playing the Tapping Game again so they can practice getting to 0 faster.

4.   Varying the "kickoff" and "focus phrase" to fit the circumstance, use the Tapping Game as much as you can to help the children focus on learning and improve their behavior.

5.   Naturally, individual children will get upset over one thing or another at different times. If you have the opportunity, you might do the Tapping Game with a child individually, focusing on the circumstance at hand. For example, if one child is very angry (8) at another, you can use the kickoff "Even though I'm really mad at _____ for _____, I like myself and I'm okay." Focus phrase: "(Name of other child)" or some other short phrase that sums up the situation.

The Tapping Game is based on Emotional Freedom Techniques® developed by Gary Craig. See http://www.emofree.com for more information.

Notes

Activity 40

How Colors Make Us Feel

Purpose of this activity: Colors have different vibrations that affect how we feel when we are around them. The purpose of this activity is to develop a greater awareness of the colors around us, how they make us feel, and how we can use colors to our advantage.

Timeframe: 15-30 minutes

What you need: no materials needed

What to do:

1. Have the children stop whatever they are doing and either sit or stand quietly in place.

2. Give the children one minute to observe and become aware of all of the colors around them (indoors or outdoors).

3. Seat the children in a circle. Ask them what colors they saw. Have the children check in to see how they feel individually right now. If that feeling had a color, what color would it be? Share with the children that different colors can make us feel different ways—especially if there's a lot of one color. Colors can make us feel calm, energized, restless, joyful, peaceful, and many other ways. Ask the children to close their eyes and picture a blue sky. How does it make them feel? What if the sky were a bright red? Would that feel different? How? Have them picture a big, grassy-green lawn. How does that feel? A bright red fire truck? A field of yellow daffodils? How do they think they'd feel if they had to wear all black all the time? All blue? All red? All yellow?

4. Explain that, generally, there are warm colors (reds, yellows, oranges) and cool colors (blues, greens, purples). The warm colors—especially the bright ones—tend to make us feel energized. Therefore, you wouldn't want your bedroom to be red, or it might be difficult to sleep in there. The cool colors tend to calm us down, so blue or some other cool color would be a better choice for a bedroom. Bright colors are fun to have in a playroom. A combination of different colors can help us feel balanced.

5. Encourage the children to identify the colors used in their homes and in their bedrooms. Later discuss how different rooms made them feel. Suggest that they become more conscious of the colors in their various environments. Brainstorm ways to use colors to help them with their feelings and moods, and see how creative everyone can be.

Notes

Activity 41

What Colors Do I Wear?

Purpose of this activity: The colors we wear can affect our moods, and they might also say something about our personalities. The purpose of this activity is for the children to become aware of the colors in the clothes they wear and how these colors may be affecting the way they feel. It's recommended that you do the previous activity first, so the children will be more familiar with the effects of colors.

Timeframe: about five minutes

What you need: no materials needed

What to do:

1. Have the children stop whatever they are doing and either sit or stand quietly in place.

2. Ask them to mentally note the colors they are wearing.

3. Have the children identify any feeling/s or qualities associated with the one or more colors they are wearing, such as calmness with blue or green, energy with red or orange, and peacefulness with pink or purple.

4. Ask them to look at their clothes when they get home to see what colors they are. Do they have a lot of clothes that are one particular color? Do they have a variety of colors in their clothes? Do they prefer to wear certain colors over others? Do they have a lot of dark colors as opposed to light colors or vice versa?

5. If age appropriate, encourage the children to choose a different color shirt or blouse and/or pants for each of the next three days. Tell them to pay attention to how each color makes them feel. Check in with them after three days, and ask if they thought they were affected by the colors they wore and what the differences were.

6. Encourage the children to pay attention to the colors they wear so they can choose something bright and cheery if they are down or something more subdued if they are feeling restless. Tell them to keep experimenting to see how colors affect them.

Notes

Activity 42

Feelings in Animals and People

Purpose of this activity: Many animals display emotions—especially those that are on the upper end of the evolutionary scale. In this activity, children will learn to appreciate their connection with animals through understanding that animals have emotions, too. In the process, they will gain empathy for animals and come to better understand their own emotions and their uniqueness on the evolutionary scale.

Timeframe: about 45 minutes, depending on the size of the group. Time is extended if the children research animals.

What you need: chalkboard, whiteboard, or flipchart and the appropriate writing utensils

What to do:

1. Ask the children in your group to tell you what kind of pets they have at home. For the children who do not have pets, ask them what their favorite animal is. Make a list of all the animals the children name.

2. Lead the children in a discussion about how different animals show that they are happy, sad, excited, tired, mad, scared, and affectionate. If they don't know how a particular animal expresses feelings, ask the child (if old enough) to research the animal in the library to find out. For younger children, you might choose an animal or two and research the animal(s) as a class. (Elephants and wolves have definitive ways of expressing their varied emotions and would be good examples to research.)

3. Compare the way animals express feelings to the way children express feelings by creating a chart. Ask the children to help you fill it in. See the following example. When the children have exhausted their ideas, you can add ideas of your own or those from the example that no one has mentioned.

4. Discuss how animals are similar to us and how they are different.

Notes

FEELING	WAYS ANIMALS SHOW IT	WAYS CHILDREN SHOW IT
Happy	**Dog:** Wags tail, plays, may bark, is friendly, may curl up at someone's feet **Cat:** Purrs, plays, or may curl up in a lap **Bird:** Sings	Smiles, laughs, can be calm and peaceful or talkative and friendly, body is relaxed
Sad	**Dog:** May whimper, not eat, lies around, has sad eyes, sleeps more than usual **Cat:** May not eat, lies around, doesn't purr **Bird:** May not eat or chatter much or have much energy	Cries, mopes, may not talk much, doesn't smile, laugh, or play, may not eat much or may eat too much, may have trouble sleeping or sleep too much, may not do well in school because can't concentrate
Scared	**Dog:** May whimper, run and hide—or freeze, may shake, wet, and bark or bite if can't get away, body gets tense, breathing gets shallow, eyes widen, may run to owner **Cat:** May meow, hide, ears may go back, eyes widen, may hiss, scratch, and bite if can't get away, body gets tense, breathing gets shallow, eyes widen **Bird:** Flutters wings, tries to fly away, will peck if can't get away	May cry or eyes may widen, may shake, may run and hide—or freeze, body gets tense, breathing gets shallow, may run to grownup
Excited	**Dog:** Barks and jumps around **Cat:** Tail whips back and forth, may run around **Bird:** Chatters and may quickly hop or fly around	Talks fast, gestures with arms and hands, may jump or move around quickly

Activity 43

Expanding Empathy

Purpose of this activity: A well-developed sense of empathy is helpful in balancing a child's social and emotional interactions. To help children understand the perspective of another, this activity begins by first having them imagine how animals feel in certain situations. It then expands to how other children or adults may feel in various circumstances.

Timeframe: about 30-45 minutes, depending on the number of questions presented and the length of sharing and discussion. This activity could also be presented in 15-minute timeframes in several sessions, dividing up the questions.

What you need: no materials needed

What to do:

1. Tell the children they are going to use their imagination and put themselves in the place of various animals in different situations to see if they can imagine how that animal feels or what that animal is experiencing.

2. Stopping after each question for the children to imagine and to get their answers, ask them:

    "How would it feel to be …

    … a gerbil in a cage?

    … a bird flying high on a sunny, calm day? On a windy day? When it's raining?

    … a bird that's hurt its wing and can't fly?

    … a doe walking with her fawn in the woods?

    … an elephant performing in a circus? Walking in the jungle?

    … a hungry mountain lion about to pounce on a rabbit to eat?

    … the rabbit?

    … a dog living with a loving family? Living with a family that fights all the time?

    … a fish swimming in a goldfish bowl? In the ocean?

    … a bear sleeping in its den? Trying to catch a fish in a stream?"

3. Explain that we really can't know what an animal is feeling, because we are people, but we can imagine how we would feel in that situation. Tell the children that now you'd like them to imagine how other people feel in certain situations. Again, stop between questions to give them time to

imagine, and ask for volunteers to explain how they would feel. Make the questions appropriate for the age of the children. Possibilities include:

"How would it feel to be …

… a hungry baby?

… a girl whose brother took a favorite thing of hers without asking?

… a boy who loves to cook and makes a great meal for his family and everyone loves it?

… a mom who made a good lunch for her child, who didn't eat most of it?

… a mom who gets stuck in a traffic jam driving home from work?

… a girl who has taken really good care of her pet hamster, and it dies?

… a boy who has taken really good care of his rabbit, and it wins a prize at the state fair?

… a child playing with a dog?

… a boy whose dad yells at him a lot?

… a dad whose children don't want to help him with anything?

… a girl who has practiced and practiced gymnastics and wins a competition?

… a child who never gets enough to eat? Has only two sets of clothes to wear?

… a boy who is out with his friends and buys a big ice cream cone, and the ice cream falls off onto his shirt and then onto the ground?"

4.   Ask the children what they learned from imagining themselves in another person's shoes.

Notes

Activity 44

Reading Facial Clues

Purpose of this activity: Facial expressions are one of the main ways we communicate our feelings to others and "read" how others are feeling. The purpose of this activity is to have children experience how our facial expressions give clues about what we are feeling at a given time and to practice "reading" emotional/social cues from others through facial expressions.

Timeframe: about 15-30 minutes depending upon the number of emotions you use

What you need: slips of paper on which you have either written an emotion (e.g., sad) or drawn a facial expression of an emotion (these are also available commercially or can be taken from magazines)

What to do:

1. Explain to the children that for this activity they will be working with partners to practice giving and reading emotional clues through facial expressions.

2. Have available several slips of paper with one emotion word or picture on each. Start out with the more common emotions such as: happy, sad, angry, puzzled, calm, upset. You can repeat this activity several times and keep adding different emotions.

3. Have the children choose a partner (or you can assign partners).

4. Circulate among the pairs of children and give one child in each pair a slip of paper, cautioning them not to let their partners see what is written or drawn on the slip of paper they receive. Then, tell the children holding the slips of paper that they are the "feelers," because they will try to help their partners, the "observers," guess the emotions they have on their slips of paper by giving facial expressions as clues.

5. Next, have the "feelers" become "observers" and vice versa. Collect the first round of slips of papers and redistribute them to the new "feelers" to act out the given emotions through facial expressions only. This time, the new "observers" must guess what the emotions are.

6. Continue the process until the children have expressed and received four to six different emotions, depending on the age/s of the children.

7. To end this activity, collect all the slips of paper. Then ask for children to voluntarily share what this activity was like for them and what they learned about getting emotional cues from people's facial expressions.

8. Point out that knowing how others are feeling can help us get along better with them, because we can respond more appropriately to their emotions.

9. To extend this activity further, ask the children which facial expressions representing which emotions had a positive effect on them and which had a negative effect on them. Encourage the children to further practice "reading" emotional cues by observing the children and adults around

them and trying to guess how those people are feeling about what they are doing or what is happening at the time.

Notes

Activity 45

Mirroring Body Language

Purpose of this activity: Mirroring another person's movements helps one to practice "reading" another person's "body language." This process also requires that one person lead and the other follow. The purpose of this activity is to give children a context in which they can learn to read another person's body language through mirroring, while at the same time being aware of what it is like to be a leader and what it is like to be a follower.

Timeframe: 15-30 minutes

What you need: adequate space for the children to move about comfortably

What to do:

1.   Start this activity by asking the question: "What do you see when you look in a mirror? Allow the children to respond spontaneously.

2.   Summarize the children's responses orally, and then tell them the activity they will be doing will be somewhat like looking in a mirror. However, instead of looking at themselves in a mirror, they will stand in front of partners, watch their partners' body movements closely, and mirror, or copy, their partners' actions.

3.   Before the children begin their partner work, demonstrate the idea of mirroring by asking the children to stand, face you, observe the movements that your body makes, and then follow along with you. Movements could include the following:

Take a step forward with your right foot.
Take a step forward with your left foot.
Raise both hands above you.
Bend over to touch your knees.
Make a figure eight in front of you with your right arm.
Make a figure eight in front of you with your left arm.
Make a quarter right turn with your body.
Make a quarter left turn with your body.
Hop on your right foot.
Hop on your left foot.

4.   When you complete this demonstration, ask the children if they have any questions, or if they wish to make any comments about what this experience was like for them.

5.   Instruct the children to choose a partner and decide who is going to be a one and who is going to be a two. With younger children, you may want to assign them partners and numbers.

6.   Tell the ones they are going to be the leaders this time, just as you were the leader for the whole group. Remind them the movements you did are only suggestions, and they can make up as many

new movements as they want. Remind the twos that they are the followers, and they are to mirror the movements of their partners as closely as possible. Give them three minutes to do this.

7. After three minutes, have the twos become the leaders and the ones become the followers. Again, stop the activity after three minutes. Adjust this time according to the ages of the children, shortening the time for younger children and lengthening the time for older children. If you wish to extend this activity, the children can do another round with their partners, change partners, or combine groups so that one person is leading and three are following. You might also have the ones act out different emotions for the twos to mirror.

8. When the mirroring movements have been completed, have the children join you in a circle or other appropriate arrangement to get their feedback about what they experienced. In addition to asking for general responses, you can guide the discussion with such questions as:

What was it like to be a leader? A follower?

How was this experience like looking in a mirror? How was it different?

Why is it important to be able to read body language?

If they haven't mirrored emotions, you can ask: Do you think children and adults express their emotions, or feelings, through body language? Give me some examples.

If they have mirrored emotional body language, you can ask: Did mirroring the other person's emotional body language help you understand what they were feeling—or, in this case, pretending to feel?

What else can you tell about a person by reading body language?

9. Conclude this activity by asking the children how they might apply what they learned today to their everyday lives.

Notes

Activity 46

Making Emotional Connections

Purpose of this activity: Emotional connections are key to our survival, to sharing love, and to experiencing the joys and challenges of our lives. The purpose of this activity is to provide children with a structure to help them become more aware of their emotional connections and how important these connections are in their everyday lives.

Timeframe: 30-45 minutes

What you need: for each child, one Appendix Activity 17 and markers of various colors

What to do:

1. Give each child Appendix Activity 17, which includes a diagram of concentric circles.

    Explain to the children that they will use the circles to identify (name) the different people in their lives. Give the following directions for how to use the circles, allowing the children time to complete each step:

    A. Choose one color of marker and write your name in the middle of the center circle.

    B. Now, with the same color in the same circle, write the names of the people you love who are closest to you, such as your mom, dad, sister/s, brother/s, grandparents, and other close family members.

    C. Next, choose another color, and in the second circle write the names of people you like and who are important to you but whom you aren't quite as close to as your family.

    D. Then, move on to the third circle and choose a third color. In this circle, write the names of people who play more minor roles in your life and whom you don't see as often but still care about and want to have in your life.

2. After the children have completed the three rings of their concentric circles, ask them to share one thing they learned about themselves with regard to the people they love and those who are important to them. Point out that being aware of these circles of emotional connection helps us know whom to go to when we need love, when we need someone to talk to, or when we need someone to help us make decisions, and whom to seek out when we need to laugh and have fun.

    You may choose to stop the activity with this "knowingness," or go on to #3 now, or do #3 as a follow-up activity in the near future.

3. Give each child a copy of the following incomplete sentences, which are on a reproducible form in the Appendix (second page of Activity 17). Have the children complete each of the sentences using the same colored markers they did in #2. (You could have younger children respond orally to one sentence at a time.)

If I needed a hug, I would go to _____

If I needed help to solve a problem, I would go to _____

If I got scared, I would want to be with _____

If I wanted to talk with someone, I would go to _____

If I wanted to laugh and play, I would choose to be with _____

(More incomplete sentences are on the Appendix form.)

4.   If children have difficulty filling in any of the blanks, remind them to look at the names they listed in their circles for ideas. If a child didn't name anyone in some categories, you may want to meet with the child at another time and see if, together, you can identify people or clarify what to do if the child has a need but no one to fill it.

5.   Remind the children that the circles they completed will keep changing as they meet new people and have different experiences. If you will be seeing these children over a period of time, collect their circles and repeat this exercise every few months to help them understand the dynamic nature of their lives and see how emotional connections change and grow.

Notes

Activity 47

Creating a Peace Place

Purpose of this activity: Children need an environment that encourages peace in order to be grounded and peaceful. This activity presents the idea of creating a Peace Place—a corner or part of the room where they can go either by themselves to enjoy the peace or with others to resolve a conflict peacefully. (See Activities 48 and 49 for processes of conflict resolution.)

Timeframe: The Peace Place can be created over time and changed periodically to keep it fresh. This activity, which introduces children to the Peace Place, takes about 15 minutes.

What you need: a place in the room that can be set aside for the purpose of peace and peacemaking, decorated with calming colors (blues, greens, lavender, purple). The Peace Place could have:

- two comfortable chairs
- big pillows or beanbags
- peaceful pictures of nature
- mandalas
- natural objects, such as interesting rocks, feathers, bark, leaves
- perhaps a goldfish bowl (with goldfish, of course)
- maybe a fountain
- books that promote peace
- a "talking stick" (see Activity 52)
- a group Peace Journal for recording ideas for how to resolve conflicts, solve problems, and interact peacefully (Activity 51)
- a CD player with headphones and CDs of peaceful music
- a folding screen or trellis to set the Peace Place apart (if budget allows)

If you want to have the children make a poster of the Peace Place Pointers (see below) and/or a Peace Place sign or banner, you will need poster board and/or banner paper and writing/drawing utensils to write and decorate them.

What to do:

1. Explain the purpose of the Peace Place to the children. Tell them it is a place where they can go if they feel the need to calm down, unwind, or relax.

2. Talk about the way the Peace Place is set up to be a peaceful environment and tell them about the different items you have placed there, or …

3. If the children are old enough, have them help you set up the Peace Place and bring some of the items. You may need to send a note home to parents to make this happen. If you get lots of items, you can switch them periodically.

4. Never use the Peace Place for time out as punishment. It should be a place where children go voluntarily to enjoy the quiet time or to write in the Group Peace Journal how they have peacefully resolved issues, solved problems, or gotten along with others in cooperative, respectful ways.

5. Establish Peace Place Pointers, i.e., rules that are positively stated, such as:

   • Keep Peace Place visitors to three (or __) at one time.
   • Keep the Peace Place tidy.
   • Use a quiet voice, if you must use one at all.
   • Move about quietly.

   Have the children help you establish these pointers. Write them on a poster (or have a child do it who has good handwriting), and have the children each draw a design or picture in the margin, creating a frame. Hang the pointers in the Peace Place.

6. If you like, have the children make a Peace Place sign or banner, which everyone could help decorate.

Notes

Activity 48

Resolving Conflicts Peacefully

Purpose of this activity: It is helpful to have a process for resolving conflicts peacefully. Once children learn and practice this process, it will become a tool for life. Providing this process is the purpose of this activity.

Timeframe: about 30 to 45 minutes

What you need: a spinner, a poster board, and markers

What to do:

1. Explain to the children that you will show them a way they can make peace with each other when they have fights, arguments, or problems. Ask them why they think making peace is important. If necessary, remind them that resolving conflicts peacefully is a great skill to have in life. If everyone knew how to do it, we wouldn't have wars, which would be a major advancement for humankind.

2. If you have established a Peace Place (Activity 47), they will know that this is the place to go in the classroom (or at home) to resolve conflicts, or make peace with each other. However, they can follow this process on the playground or anywhere else they happen to be.

3. Go over the following steps of settling conflicts peacefully:

    A. Each child involved in the conflict take turns explaining what happened and how it made him/her feel. Use a spinner to determine who goes first—i.e., the child nearest to where the spinner ends up pointing. (If the children are outside the classroom, the person whose first name comes first in the alphabet can go first.)

    B. Each child gets to respond to what the other has said. (In the Peace Place, a "talking stick" can be used to facilitate this interaction. See Activity 52 for an explanation of talking sticks and how to make them.)

    C. Both children (or all involved) must agree to end the disagreement or conflict between them in the interest of establishing a more comfortable peace.

    D. Each child offers one suggestion as to how they can avoid getting into such a conflict again.

4. Help the children role play various situations of possible conflict so they understand the process and internalize it. (For a while, you may need to supervise the process as the need occurs. Later, the children may be able to handle it themselves.)

5. The conflict resolution procedure above can be abbreviated, written on a poster board (decorated, if desired), and posted in the Peace Place, once the children understand the process. A possible abbreviation is:

A. Spin to see who talks first.
B. Take turns explaining what happened and how you feel.
C. Respond to each other.
D. Agree to end the conflict peacefully.
E. Each person offer a suggestion on how to avoid such conflicts.

Note: This activity can be combined with Activity 49, Resolving Conflicts with POOF!

"The choice between love and fear is made every moment in our hearts and minds. That is where the peace process begins. Without peace within, peace in the world is an empty wish. Like love, peace is extended. It cannot be brought from the world to the heart. It must be brought from each heart of another, and thus to all mankind."

Paul Ferrini

Notes

Activity 49

Resolving Conflicts with POOF!

Purpose of this activity: When conflicts arise, we can be tempted to lash out, blame the other/s involved, or even express our anger physically if we haven't been taught another way to deal with conflicts. This activity provides another, more balanced way to approach these situations. The purpose is to have the children learn this approach early, so they'll find that their conflicts go POOF! more quickly.

Timeframe: about 45 minutes

What you need: a chalkboard and chalk or a flipchart and colored markers; materials to make POOF! wands, including one ¼-inch dowel the length of a wand, one large cotton ball, and four, precut, 6-inch ribbon streamers in different colors for each child; and glue

What to do:

1. Make a sample POOF! wand before you introduce this activity: Glue one end of each of four ribbon streamers onto one end of a wand-size dowel so the streamers hang down different sides of the dowel. Then, glue a large cotton ball on the end of the wand on top of the glued ribbon ends.

2. Gather the children so that everyone can see the chalkboard or flipchart. Hold a discussion about what it's like for them when they are angry with others or have disagreements. Ask volunteers to share times when conflicts have occurred in their lives. How did they feel? How did the conflicts get resolved?

3. Tell the children that there is a way called POOF! that they can resolve these situations more quickly.

   - Write OO on the board (or flipchart). Tell the children that this is the way it feels when we have conflicts and we don't know how to deal with them. Oo, they can hurt!

   - Add a P at the beginning and an F at the end to make POOF. (Then add an exclamation mark.)

     Explain to everyone that in a conflict situation, the P stands for "Pay attention to the Problem." This means they need to stick to talking about the Problem and how to solve it rather than blaming the other person involved. Blaming doesn't help the situation. An intention to solve the problem peacefully does.

     The F stands for "Focus on Feelings." This means that it's okay, and even good, to say how you feel when you have a fight or a problem or conflict. Always start with "I feel ...." That way you can stay away from blame and not make the other person more angry. The other person might try to argue about anything else you say, but your feelings are your feelings, and no one can argue that you don't feel that way. Likewise, however, the other person should have the chance to say how he or she feels.

4. Explain that if we Pay attention to the Problem and Focus on Feelings, the OO becomes a good OO, as in "Oo, that feels better!" Then, POOF! Your conflict disappears.

5. Practice POOF! on a few hypothetical conflicts. Help the children role play the conflicts so they can get a feel for what to say and how to react when real conflicts arise. For example, suppose Jimmy has taken Sarah's marker.

Old way:
Sarah: "You took my red marker, you thief!"
Jimmy: "Too bad! I need a red one, and now I have it. Ha Ha!"
Sarah: "Teacher! Jimmy took my marker!"

POOF! way:
Sarah: "I'm mad that you took my marker. Now I can't finish my picture."
Jimmy: "Well, I need a red one, too, and there aren't enough to go around."
Sarah: "Let's go ask the teacher to find another red marker. If we can't find another one, then as soon as I'm finished with my picture, you can use it."
Jimmy: "I was ready to use red and I don't want to wait."
Sarah: "Let's just ask."
Jimmy: "Okay, we'll ask the teacher. If he can't find another red one, I guess I can use the green one until you're done with the red."

6. After the children have role played a few situations, have them sit down and ask for volunteers to pass out the materials to make POOF! wands. The wands will remind the children to POOF! their conflicts away. You might keep your sample wand in the Peace Place, if you have established one, perhaps alongside the talking stick, as they are both tools for balance and peace.

Note: You might want to combine this activity with Activity 48, Resolving Conflicts Peacefully, or do the two activities on consecutive days.

Notes

Activity 50

Creating Personal Peace Journals

Purpose of this activity: Putting thoughts onto paper helps children process and retain ideas. In this activity, the children create personal peace journals to help them think about and better understand how they can help themselves be more balanced and peaceful.

Timeframe: Journals can be made in about 45 minutes. Recording in them can be spread over time, with the children recording their thoughts (see below) at different times.

What you need: five sheets of white, 8½-by-11-inch paper and one sheet of 8½-by-11-inch pastel construction paper per child, ribbon or yarn (or stapler) for binding, and drawing and writing utensils

What to do:

1. Have the children fold the white paper and the construction paper in half so their journals will be 5½ by 8½ inches. Have them tie the pages together with a ribbon or yarn wrapped around the crease and tied in a bow on the outside. If you prefer, staple the crease in three places with a stapler that opens and can be used that way.

2. Tell the children to title their books My Peace Journal, and have each child write his or her name on the front. They may decorate the front of their Peace Journals however they wish. (Young children may need help with the writing.) Ask them to use pictures or designs and colors that remind them of peace.

3. You may have the children write in their journals at any time. You might want to have them start by writing down, thinking about, and answering the following questions. Young children can draw pictures if they cannot yet write well.

   - What does the word peace mean to me?

   - How does my body feel when it's not peaceful?
   - How does my body feel when it's peaceful?
   - What can I do to help my body feel more peaceful?

   - What kind of thoughts do I have when I'm not peaceful?
   - What kind of thoughts do I have when I'm peaceful?
   - What can I do to help my mind be more peaceful?

   - What kind of feelings do I have when I'm not peaceful?
   - What kind of feelings do I have when I'm peaceful?
   - What can I do to help my feelings be more peaceful?

4. After each session of writing in their journals, discuss the children's answers, asking for volunteers to share what they've written. Let them know that sharing can help others by giving them ideas that perhaps they hadn't thought of themselves.

5. Periodically, give the children time to write in their peace journals about whatever may be bothering them and how they can help themselves be more peaceful. You might want to emphasize that they don't have to solve all their problems themselves. They can ask an adult for help. We all need to help each other be more peaceful. That's the way to a more peaceful world.

Notes

Activity 51

Creating a Group Peace Journal

Purpose of this activity: The children will help to create a Group (or Class) Peace Journal to keep in the Peace Place (Activity 47). In this journal, they can record successful conflict resolutions, ways they have solved problems, and other ways they have discovered to get along well with others. The purpose is to raise awareness and share ideas.

Timeframe: Journal can be made in about 30 minutes. Children can start out by each recording an idea in the journal about how to better get along with others. Then, they can record their thoughts after a conflict is resolved or problem solved, or at any time they are inspired.

What you need: a three-ring binder with a clear plastic sleeve on the front, a decorative sheet of paper (on which you or one of the children will print or handwrite the title), punched and lined notebook paper (more than one sheet per child), and drawing and writing utensils

What to do:

1. Explain to the children that they will be helping to make a group peace journal to use in the Peace Place. In this journal, they can record ways in which they have successfully resolved fights or misunderstandings, ways they have solved problems, and other ways they have discovered to get along well with others. They can sign their contributions or not, as they wish. The journal will be a resource for everybody.

2. Ahead of time, create or have one of the children create the title page of the Group (or Class) Peace Journal on decorative paper. (Or the children can decorate the paper.) Slide the page into the front plastic sleeve of the notebook you will use for the peace journal.

3. Show the notebook to all the children and explain its purpose. Give each child a sheet of lined, punched paper, and tell the children you'd like them all to get the group journal started by writing one idea about how to stay peaceful with others or how to peacefully resolve differences with others.

4. When everyone is finished, conduct a discussion, asking volunteers to share what they've written.

5. Collect the papers, and put them in the notebook along with blank (but lined) sheets that can be used at a later time.

6. Put the notebook in the Peace Place, and tell the childen to use it when they feel inspired or want to share ideas for resolving conflicts and getting along with others. They may write on any of the pages that still have room to write.

Notes

Activity 52

Creating Talking Sticks

Purpose of this activity: The "talking stick" is a Native American tradition. It is a decorated stick used in a ceremonial way to maintain order during group discussions and show respect for everyone's thoughts and feelings. It is a way to create peace. In this activity, each child has the opportunity to make a talking stick to take home and use in a family setting. In addition, all can participate in creating a talking stick for the class or group—or you can create one ahead of time to show the group as an example and use with the group later.

Timeframe: about 45 minutes.

What you need: a sturdy, fairly straight stick* for each child (or have them each bring one in), paint and brushes (or markers), ribbons, perhaps leather or suede strips (such as leather shoelaces), feathers, "jewels," or small, decorative rocks, beads, shells, and/or other decorations, as well as scissors and glue for each child

*It is easier to paint the stick if it has no bark on it, but bark is optional. A good size is about 1½-2 feet long and about an inch or two in diameter. If you ask the children to bring in sticks, show them an appropriate one as an example, and give them at least several days to find ones they like.

What to do:

1. Explain the purpose of a talking stick to the children (see above). Whoever holds the stick is allowed to speak without interruption from anyone else in the group but must speak truthfully, from the heart. The rest should listen from their hearts, without thinking about what they are going to say when it comes to them.

    Tell the children that, for group discussions, they will sit in a circle and the talking stick will be passed clockwise around the circle, giving each person the opportunity to speak—or to pass. In some situations, the talking stick can be kept in the middle of the group. When someone wants to talk, he or she picks up the stick. When the speaker is finished, he or she returns the talking stick to its place for the next person who wishes to speak.

    Show the children the ceremonial way to hold the talking stick, with two hands underneath it.

2. Tell the children they can each make a talking stick to take home (and help make one for the group, if that is what you decide to do).

3. Give each child a stick (or have them use sticks they found themselves). Have the paint and brushes or markers, scissors, glue, ribbons, and other decorations available. Tell the children they can decorate their talking sticks however they like.

4. If the children are helping to decorate the group talking stick, have them take turns adding one thing to the group stick in between tasks on their own sticks.

5. When the sticks are finished and after everything has dried (perhaps the next day), get together in a circle. Have each child tell about his/her talking stick, using the group talking stick to take turns so they can see how it works. Make sure everyone who wants to talk has the opportunity.

6. Tell the children to take their talking sticks home and try them out with family discussions.

Notes

Activity 53

Counting Thoughts, Calming Down

Purpose of this activity: This activity is short but very effective. Its purpose is to calm down the body, mind, and emotions. In the resulting state of calm, learning is more effective, and behavior improves.

Timeframe: up to five minutes

What you need: no materials needed

What to do:

1. This short activity can be done either sitting or standing, but sitting is preferable, as the activity is very relaxing.

2. Ask the children to either close their eyes or focus on a spot on the floor.

3. Tell them they have ___ minutes to just count their thoughts. (Determine how long you can reasonably expect your group to be able to do this. Even two or three minutes may be enough to calm the mind and emotions and relax the body.) Explain that as a thought comes into their minds, count it, let it go, and wait for the next thought. Tell the children not to hop on a train of thought and take a ride, but to let it go on past, waiting for the next … and the next…. They are not to judge the thoughts as good or bad—just thoughts to count.

4. When the time is up, ask the children to tell you how many thoughts they counted, and record the numbers on a sheet of paper. Ask the children what happened as they counted their thoughts. (Typically, when you're waiting for thoughts to come so they can be counted, your thoughts slow down. See if anyone mentions this phenomenon. You might want to eventually ask if anyone experienced it.)

5. Try this activity periodically and see how the numbers of thoughts change. The thoughts may become fewer and fewer as the children become better at watching for their thoughts, counting them, and letting them go. Naturally, however, it will be more difficult to count thoughts on some days than others. At times, the mind seems to race, or there's a greater tendency to hop on trains of thought and get carried away than at other times. Tell the children not to judge themselves when this happens. Make the activity a game to see how the mind works and how patiently the children can wait and count.

Notes

Activity 54

Labyrinth Adventure

Purpose of this activity: Walking a labyrinth helps calm the mind—and slowly tracing such a winding, repetitive path can have a similar effect. It also can improve hand-eye coordination and concentration. Add counting turns, and you have another level of difficulty involving focus and memory. Add drawing, and you have imagination and creativity. Thus, besides calming the mind (and body), this activity helps balance the right and left parts of the brain.

Timeframe: about 10 minutes

What you need: one Appendix Activity 18 per child, markers (or crayons) in different colors, a CD of soft music, and a CD player (or tape and a tape player)

What to do:

1. Give each child a copy of the labyrinth (Appendix Activity 18) and three markers (or crayons) of different colors.

2. Tell the children they are going to travel slowly into the labyrinth (using a marker or crayon), counting the turns they take on their journey. They will find something of great value at the center, which they must imagine and draw when they get there. They must use one color going in to the center, another to draw their pictures, and yet another color coming back out. They must remember how many turns they took going in while they draw and continue the counting where they left off when they start back to the outside of the labyrinth. (You needn't have young children count. For the older children, it adds another level of challenge and focus.)

3. Play soft music while the children journey through their labyrinths.

4. When everyone is finished, ask how many turns they took. Did everyone get the same number? Ask for volunteers to explain what they found at the center and show their drawings.

5. You might do this activity periodically and give the children a different assignment for when they reach the center. ("When you reach the center, you find the most beautiful flower in the world. Imagine and draw that flower." "When you reach the center, you find a friendly dragon who grants you a wish. Imagine and draw that dragon—and make your wish!")

Notes

Activity 55

Make Like a Tree and Ground Yourself

Purpose of this activity: This visualization activity helps children ground themselves when they are feeling flighty or restless or unable to focus.

Timeframe: less than five minutes

What you need: no materials needed

What to do:

1. Have the children stop what they are doing, put their arms out to their sides, stand firmly with their legs slightly apart, and close their eyes (or focus on one spot on the floor).

2. Tell them to pretend they are trees with sturdy trunks. Ask them to picture their roots going deep, deep into the ground. A main tap root grows straight down from each tree, and smaller roots fan out from this large root, creating a web of roots beneath the tree that helps its trunk to be solid and strong.

3. Tell the "trees" that a gentle breeze has come along and is blowing through their leaves, making their trunks sway just a bit and their branches slightly wave. But the trees' roots hold them steady.

4. Ask the trees to imagine sunlight filtering through their leaves and branches, warming their trunks.

5. Tell them that now clouds have drifted over them, and it has started to rain. Ask the trees to feel the raindrops splash on their leaves and run down their trunks—all the way to the ground and through the earth to their roots, which thirstily soak up the water.

6. Now tell the trees to imagine they are boys and girls again. They can now move their feet and open their eyes. They feel refreshed and relaxed and are ready for their next activity.

Notes

Activity 56

Creating a Friendship Space

Purpose of this activity: Friendship is a necessary part of our lives. It is through friendship that we develop emotional maturity, social skills, and a sense of belonging. Creating a space for children to connect with their friends and form new friendships encourages this emotional/social development. The purpose of this activity is to discuss and arrange for a Friendship Space to be set up in the classroom.

Timeframe: about 30 minutes. (Additional time will be required for gathering items the children decide they want in the space, setting up the space, and making—or having the children make—a poster of expected behaviors for the space, unless you wish to use the sample guidelines in the Appendix.)

What you need: a flipchart and colored markers; Appendix Activity 19, Guidelines for Creating a Friendship Space, for your own use (and possibly the Guidelines for the Friendship Space to copy and post)

What to do:

1. Discuss with the children what friendship means to them. Highlight the different aspects of friendship, such as having someone to get together with to go to a movie, play a game, go for a walk, listen to music, or talk and laugh, and having someone to comfort you when you're down or celebrate with you when you're happy.

2. Depending on your setting, discuss the importance of having a place and times to get together with friends in a variety of environments. For the purpose of this activity, a school environment will be used as an example. Remind the children that there are times in the school day, such as lunch, outside time, and recreation time that they have an opportunity to be with one or more friends. Ask them if they also would like to have some times for getting together while they are in your room. If so, then plan with the group what it will take to make this happen.

3. Ask the children what they think is needed to make it possible to have friendship times within the context of the classroom. Write their ideas on the flipchart as the children give them. Most likely, your list will include a space for getting together, materials to have available, behaviors to be expected, and possibilities for times to go to the friendship space. (See Appendix Activity 19 for ideas.) Depending on the number of children and their age/s, you might want to have them choose which of the topics they want to work on for the friendship space. Otherwise, you can work with the whole group to determine the basics for getting started.

    If working with the whole group:

    *   Discuss the possible spaces in the classroom that could be available for a friendship space, then choose the space that would be the most appropriate.

    *   List some basic materials (appropriate for the age group of the children) that could be in the friendship place.

- Discuss and list the behaviors that would be expected of those using this space to be with one or more friends. These behaviors would accommodate the children in the rest of the room who are doing things by themselves or working on an assignment. They would also accommodate children in a designated "quiet space," if you have one.

- Determine the conditions and times that this space can be used, such as when the participants' assignments are completed, during the first five minutes after they come into the room, or other times that work with the class schedule.

- Depending on the number of children in your group, you may need to decide how many children can be in this space at one time and if a sign-up sheet is needed.

4. Encourage the children to either choose friends to be in this space with them or to go to the friendship space by themselves during appropriate times. Going there alone could be viewed as an invitation for someone to join them.

5. After the friendship space has been in use for a few weeks, ask the children to come together to evaluate how this space has been working and what changes may need to be made. Suggestions for changes should come from you and the children, with the understanding that you have the final say regarding the use of the friendship space.

6. Encourage the children to consider the ideas they learned in setting up and using their friendship space when they make new friends in their neighborhoods. They also might want to expand on the kinds of activities they engage in with friends.

Notes

Activity 57

Creating a Quiet Space

Purpose of this activity: To help maintain a healthy state of balance, human beings need time and a place where they can reflect, relax, and wind down from the pressures of scheduled time and activities. This is especially important for children as they grow and learn a healthy lifestyle. The purpose of this activity is to give children the experience of creating a quiet space in a room that accommodates a variety of activities, thus providing a model for them to use in their home environments.

Timeframe: about 30 minutes. (Additional time will be required for gathering items the children decide they want in the space, setting up the space, and making—or having the children make—a poster of expected behaviors for the space, unless you wish to use the sample guidelines in the Appendix.)

What you need: paper, writing and drawing utensils for the designated recorder/s in the group/s, a flipchart or drawing board if you are working with young children, and a poster board

What to do:

1. Begin by asking the children to think about the space they have in their homes or apartments. (If you are doing this activity as a parent, keep the focus on the home rather than a school or community environment.) Ask them to name the activities involved in their daily routines at home, such as eating, playing, watching TV, and sleeping. Then ask them to think of a place in their homes where they could go if they wanted to have some quiet time to relax, listen to calming music, read, or just rest after doing many active things. By a show of hands, ask how many of them have such a place in their homes.

2. Point out to the children that it is important to have a quiet space in any location to spend some time relaxing. Before going on to #3, you might want to review the meaning of balance and how activity needs to be balanced with quietness or inactivity for our well-being.

3. Tell the children that their task for the next half hour is to: a) come up with ideas for creating a space in the classroom that can be designated as a Quiet Space, b) brainstorm a list of objects that could be included in this space, and c) decide what behavior will be expected of anyone using this space. With older children, you may want to create three groups to cover each of the three components of this task. You can ask for volunteers for each group to allow for individual interests, or simply count off by threes to form the groups. If you are working with younger children or have a small group, you may want to do all three components as one group. Note: for ideas about objects to include in this space, refer to Activity 47, Creating a Peace Place. That activity is similar to this one, except that the Peace Place is also a place to resolve conflicts. Also refer to Appendix Activity 20 for other ideas about creating a Quiet Space.

4. Depending on the age group and how much time you'd like to spend, take about 10-15 minutes for the group as a whole or the three groups to work on the components of the task. If in one group, record the group's thoughts on the flipchart or board, or if you have three groups, have one person in each group record his or her group's thoughts on paper (either in writing or drawings).

5. At the end of the designated time, if you have small groups, have them come together to share their ideas. Then, as a whole group, decide where in the room the space is going to be (as free from distractions as possible and away from a high-traffic pattern), the objects to have available in the space, and the behaviors expected when someone uses this space. Ask for volunteers to create a poster listing these behaviors to put up in the space. (A sample poster of guidelines is included in Appendix Activity 20.)

6. Within the next few days, create the Quiet Space for the children, or ask who would like to help you. This would be an opportunity for the children to learn how to create such a space in their homes or other community environments.

7. When the space is set up, talk about when it can be used, and review the behaviors expected while in this space.

8. Encourage the children to note how they feel after using this space, and periodically check in with them after they have had the chance to use it. Does it help them rebalance to go on to other activities with more energy and focus? Encourage them to create a similar space at home, and suggest that they invite other family members to use this space when they need a calming and quiet time.

Notes

Section 3

Nourishing the Spirit

Activity 58

Being in Nature

Purpose of this activity: Being in nature can bring us joy, serenity, and a greater degree of balance, and it nourishes our spirit (a sense of the sacred). The purpose of this activity is to learn about nature by connecting with it through our senses and careful observation.

Timeframe: about 30 minutes to one hour (depending on the age/s of the children and how many parts of this activity you choose to do) plus the time it takes to walk or travel to the nature area

What you need: a safe, natural place such as a park, conservation area, or beach; a backpack for each child to carry a mat to sit on, art materials, a journal, and a pen. For older children, you might want to add a book for identifying birds and/or plants in your area.

What to do:

1. Choose a natural site to go to with the children. If there is not one within walking distance, plan for a time when you can take a field trip to such a site, which will extend the required time but could result in a fun and meaningful adventure.

2. Have the children pack the materials needed for the outing. Bring a snack, if appropriate (and add the time it will take to have it).

3. When you get to the site, have each child choose a special spot to sit. Tell the children to sit as still as possible and just watch and listen. Suggest they watch for small animals and birds and observe the sand (if at the beach) or earth and vegetation around them. Have them listen carefully to see if they can pick up bird, animal, wind, or water sounds. Ask them to smell the air. Can they smell the vegetation? The water? Anything else? If appropriate, have them touch the natural objects around them. Are they hard? Smooth? Rough? Warm from the sun?

4. If this is the first time the children have done this type of activity, 10 minutes of observation will probably be enough for younger children and about 20 minutes for older children. Then have them journal what the saw, heard, and felt. (Or, depending on the age/s of the children, you may wish to have them just talk about their experiences.) When they have finished journaling or discussing, ask them if this experience called up any memories. You might want to suggest the children write (or tell) about their memories, or you could have them write a story from the point of view of an animal they saw. (Depending on your available time, you could have them do this after they return to the classroom or home.)

5. Next have the children draw a picture of whatever interests them, which might be the whole scene or a detail, such as a leaf or an anthill. When you're ready to go, have them clean up their spots and pack their backpacks. Make sure nothing is left behind. Make a point of cleaning up and not littering to maintain the beauty of the natural environment.

6. When you arrive back at your place of origin, have the children verbally share their experiences of being in nature (if they have not already done so), read what they wrote in their journals, or share their pictures.

7. Ask the children how they felt before their connection with the natural environment and how they feel now as a result of their experience. Encourage the children to do this activity again with a friend or their families, pointing out that connecting with nature can help us feel more calm and peaceful, and it is a delightful way to learn more about our natural environment.

Notes

Activity 59

Patterns in a Fingerprint

Purpose of this activity: Many patterns exist in nature, including those in our bodies. In this activity, the children will observe the patterns in their fingerprints. Thus children will increase their sense of connection with nature and its patterns. They also will enhance their appreciation for their own uniqueness. As in the other activities about patterns in nature, children will fine-tune their observation and focusing skills, which, in turn, will help them to slow down and enjoy the finer details of life.

Timeframe: about 10 minutes

What you need: an ink pad that has washable ink (or the kind of "dry" ink pad used in banks to put thumbprints on checks), a rectangle of white, unlined paper for each child that is large enough for a fingerprint and their name below it, a wet washcloth, a dry towel, writing utensils, a large sheet of colored or black paper, a glue stick

What to do:

1. Have the children bring their pieces of paper up to the ink pad, roll their index fingers on the pad, and stamp their fingerprints on their papers. They can wash and dry their fingers on the washcloth and towel. (The ink from "dry" ink pads just wipes off.)

2. Ask the children to sit and observe their own prints carefully. Have them note the swirls and patterns.

3. Have each child compare his or her print with a neighbor's print. How are the two fingerprints the same? How are they different?

4. The children can put their names on their individual pieces of paper and glue them onto one big sheet of paper, which can be posted to show everyone's unique prints.

Notes

Activity 60

Purposeful Patterns in Nature

Purpose of this activity: Nature manifests in many shapes, patterns, and colors. In this activity, the children will look at shapes, patterns, and colors in mammals, insects, and birds that have the purpose of camouflage. Thus, they will enhance their appreciation for the intelligence inherent in nature that creates such purposeful patterns and improve their observation and focusing skills.

Timeframe: 30 minutes

What you need: Photographs of animals or insects that have evolved patterns, coloring, shapes, and/or textures that help them survive by blending in with their environments. Examples: leaf and stick insects, fish that look like sand, butterflies or moths that look like leaves or bark, animals that turn white in winter, animals whose spots help them blend in with their surroundings, and so on.

What to do:

1. Pass the pictures around the group or show pictures in a book to the group as a whole.

2. Ask for volunteers to describe what they see in the pictures (e.g., a bug that looks like a leaf). Is it difficult to see the insect or animal? Why?

3. Ask the children if they know why these animals look like their backgrounds. Discuss the concept of camouflage as protection and the intelligence in nature that makes animals grow in certain ways to protect themselves.

4. Tell the children to be on the lookout for insects or animals that are camouflaged. They will be difficult to see!

Notes

Activity 61

Nature-Inspired Designs

Purpose of this activity: By observing and handling objects from nature that have various patterns and then creating their own designs inspired by those they have observed, children will increase their sense of connection with nature. They will enhance their appreciation for natural aesthetics and nature's creativity as well as develop their own creative abilities.

Timeframe: one hour

What you need: natural objects that have definite patterns, for example: pine cones; different kinds of bark; pieces of wood (can be cut) that show distinctive grain patterns (such as oak or pine); flowers (such as daisies, roses, or thistles); stones (such as marble); seashells; nuts (such as walnuts, whole or halved). Use your imagination. If you need to, you can gather pictures of these objects instead of the real thing, but the actual objects provide a kinesthetic experience for the children and are more interesting.

What to do:

1. Explain to the children that today they will be checking out the artwork of Mother Nature and using her designs to inspire themselves in creating artwork.

2. Pass around the natural objects you have gathered for the children to observe. Tell them to look carefully at the lines and shapes in the objects. Are the lines curved or straight? Are the shapes round, angled, or pointed? Does a pattern of lines and shapes repeat, or is it different throughout the object? Does the object have the same shape(s) on both sides (symmetrical), or are the two sides different (asymmetrical)? If you use boards of wood, ask them to look at the grain in the wood. Tell them that trees are cut in certain ways to make objects that show off the beautiful grain in the wood. Ask them to check out the furniture they have at home for the woodgrain. If you use flowers, you may want to keep them in a vase on a table and have the children go up a few at a time to look at them closely and observe their shapes and details.

3. After the children have had enough time to observe all the objects, pass out the drawing paper and crayons, markers, or other drawing tools. Tell the children to play Mother Nature and create a beautiful design using the shapes and patterns they have observed. They may combine any of the patterns in ways that they choose and use any colors.

4. When they have finished, ask the children to share their designs and talk about which natural objects they used as inspirations.

5. Encourage the children to look more carefully at objects in nature when they are out and about and appreciate Mother Nature's artwork.

Notes

Activity 62

Color Hunt

Purpose of this activity: Mother Nature displays a lavish palette of colors. This activity helps the children become more aware of the variety of colors in nature and how they coexist. It helps children appreciate variety and to learn not to judge differences. This activity also helps develop the children's aesthetic sense and appreciation of nature. Although it is best done outdoors, if circumstances aren't favorable to this, an alternate approach is suggested below.

Timeframe: about one hour

What you need: a box of crayons or markers, at least two sheets of drawing paper, and something such as a clipboard to put the paper on for drawing (or a small drawing pad) per child. (The alternative indoor activity requires magazines with a variety of colorful photographs of nature.)

What to do:

1. Plan ahead to identify a park area around your school or neighborhood, or find a nature trail to take the children for a walking hunt to look for colors that occur in nature. Pick a colorful time of year and the most colorful area that is available to you.

    If doing this activity outdoors is not practical for you, an alternative is to provide the children with magazines that have a variety of pictures of nature displaying many colors.

2. Before your walk, give each child the crayons or markers, drawing paper, and clipboard (or pad). Have the children stop periodically to record the colors they see by making small circles of all the colors. Continue this process until you reach the end of your walk. If you prefer, and depending upon the age of the children, you may have them record each new color they notice as they walk along.

    If you are doing the activity indoors, have the children go through nature magazines and do the same thing.

3. At the end of the walk, have the children find a comfortable place to sit, if appropriate for the outdoor setting you are in—or you can have the children go back indoors to do this part of the activity. Ask them to use their second sheets of paper to draw designs, images, or pictures using all of the colors they saw while on their nature walk (or in their magazines).

4. Tell the children they can use their observation skills to go on color hunts at any time in any environment. Discuss the similarities and differences between how colors occur in nature compared to how colors occur in our homes, schools, shopping malls, and other man-made environments. Pose the question, "What can the colors of nature teach us about the use of color in our everyday lives?" For older children, you may want to ask, "Can a comparison be drawn between how different colors appear in nature and how different people coexist together? How are these situations the same? How are they different?"

Dear God,
I didn't think orange went with purple until I saw the sunset you made on Tue. That was cool.

EUGENE

From *Children's Letters to God,*
compiled by Stuart Hample and Eric Marshall
(New York: Workman Publishing, 1991)

Notes

Activity 63

Trees Are Our Friends; Are We Their Friends?

Purpose of this activity: This is a short activity with a lot of potential for expansion. Its purpose is to help children become more aware of the life-giving, awe-inspiring benefits of trees and what we can do to protect these valuable resources. This awareness will, in turn, help to develop the qualities of respect, caring, and appreciation.

Timeframe: about 10 minutes. (See below for ways to extend this activity.)

What you need: no materials needed (optional: a flipchart, chalk- or whiteboard, or poster board on which to record the children's ideas)

What to do:

1. Ask the children to stop what they are doing for Tree Time. Explain that you would like to take a few minutes to honor trees. Begin by sharing the following facts:

    *   Trees are the longest-living organisms on earth.

    *   Trees are our friends because they absorb the carbon dioxide that we exhale as a waste product of our bodies and provide us with the oxygen we need to stay alive.

    *   In one year, a single tree can absorb as much carbon dioxide as a car produces driving 26,000 miles.

    *   Two mature trees can provide enough oxygen for a family of four.

    *   Trees also give us beauty, comfort from the hot sun, various fruits, and the basic material from which we make paper and building products.

2. Next, ask the children to take two minutes to think about how they can be better friends to trees by the actions they take in our everyday lives, such as: not wasting paper and paper products, recycling paper, buying recycled paper products whenever possible, planting new trees in appropriate places, and finding ways to support rain forest projects. Have the children brainstorm as many other ideas as they can.

3. Encourage the children to decide on one action they will take every month to help a tree or trees in general. Also, encourage the children to get their parents involved in this project. End the activity by pointing out that just as we are dependent upon trees to help us, trees are dependent upon us to help them. We and the trees are friends, and we are both better off when we care about each other and take actions that will benefit both of us.

4. If you wish to extend this activity for more than 10 minutes, or come back to it at another time, you can expand the idea of how trees help us, focusing on the ways that are appropriate for your age group of children. Lots of fun activities can be created around this idea, including artwork, service

projects, researching the literature for poems and essays on trees, visiting a tree farm, visiting a nature center, and inviting an arborist in to talk with the children about tree care. You might want to have Tree Time periodically throughout the year and do tree activities that relate to the seasons.

Notes

Activity 64 *(1 in a Series of 6)*

Exploring the Natural Elements Shared by Humans and Planet Earth

Purpose of this series of activities: Being in nature, observing, and connecting with the natural elements of earth (soil), water, air, and fire (energy) helps us to experience the beauty, patterns, and balance inherent in our natural environment. It also helps us balance our sense of our own nature between man-made space and natural space. As we become aware that every living thing is made from the same natural elements and is dependent upon the same elements for survival and growth, we can develop a deep sense of the interconnectedness between humans and the natural environment. This series of six activities is meant to enhance that awareness and sense of connection.

See the individual activities in the series for their purposes, timeframes, materials, and instructions. Those for the first activity are below.

The purpose of this first activity in the series is to introduce the four natural elements of planet Earth: earth (with a small e, meaning soil, or dirt), water, air, and fire.

Timeframe: The activities in this series can take place in six consecutive days (not counting the weekend), be extended over a month, adapted to fit into one day, or conducted over an indefinite period of time. The activities vary in time from about 15 minutes to an hour.

This first activity takes about 15-30 minutes.

What you need: a package of seeds (or a few seeds) and enough brown, blue, white, and red slips of paper for each child in your group to be able to choose a color (representing an element)

What to do:

1. Tell the children that today will be the beginning of a series of six activities. Explain that the purpose of this series is to learn more about the natural elements that we share with planet Earth. By becoming more aware of our shared qualities, we can better understand how the balance of these elements within our bodies and the planet creates and maintains the web of life in this world. As expressed by Luther Standing Bear in *My People, the Sioux:*

    "Dakota children understand that we are of the soil and the soil of us,
    that we love the birds and beasts that grew with us on this soil.
    A bond exists between all things because they all drink
    the same water and breathe the same air."

    (Boston: Houghton Mifflin, 1928. p. 83)

2. Ask the children to identify three of the four natural elements in the above quote. Then ask if someone can name the other element. Show the children a package of seeds or a few seeds held in your hand. Ask the children what these seeds would need to sprout and grow into plants. Answers might include:

- soil, or dirt (and, if indoors, a container for the dirt)
- water
- light (preferably natural sunlight)
- air

3. Next, ask the children what we, as humans, need to survive and grow. Bring the children to the understanding that we need the same four elements as the plants in order to survive and grow: air, water, fire (sunlight, energy), and food, which comes from the soil. Point out that plants release oxygen into the air, and oxygen is a gas that our bodies need to survive. In turn, we breathe out carbon dioxide, which is a gas that plants need to survive. So we need plants, and they need us.

4. Tell the children you would like them to see what they can discover about the four elements by exploring different resources. To begin, they each will choose (or be given) one of the elements. Their goal is to learn as much as they can about that element in the next 24 hours. Encourage them to use as many resources as they can. You might make the following suggestions, depending on the age of the children:

- people
- books and other library resources
- the Internet
- personal observation
- intuition (putting out the thought or intent of what you want information about, then waiting for an answer in the form of an image, a thought, or a feeling)

5. Next, ask the children to choose an element, giving them either a brown slip for earth, a blue slip for water, a white slip for air, or a red slip for fire. (If you like, you can randomly hand out the slips of paper or have the children draw them out of a bag or basket.)

6. Encourage the children to be as creative as possible in seeking out sources of information and to have fun discovering as much as they can about their elements. Tell them they will be sharing what they learned in the next activity. (Decide when that will be and let them know.)

"A human being is a part of the whole, called by us 'Universe,' a part limited in time and space. He experiences himself, his thoughts and feelings as something separated from the rest—a kind of optical delusion of his consciousness. This delusion is a kind of prison for us, restricting us to our personal desires and to affection for a few persons nearest to us. Our task must be to free ourselves from this prison by widening our circle of compassion to embrace all living creatures and the whole of nature in its beauty. Nobody is able to achieve this completely, but the striving for such achievement is in itself a part of the liberation and a foundation for inner security."

Albert Einstein, quoted in H. Eves' *Mathematical Circles Adieu*
(Boston: Prindle, Weber, and Schmidt, 1977)

Notes

Sharing Research on the Natural Elements

Purpose of this activity: This is the second in a series of activities designed to help children learn more about the natural elements of earth (soil), water, air, and fire (energy). In this activity the children share the knowledge they gained in researching their chosen elements. In the process, they become more familiar with the many sources of information we have available to us and they learn how to organize and record the results of their research.

Timeframe: about 30-45 minutes, depending upon the ages of the children and size of the group

What you need: a flipchart or two sheets of poster board and one Appendix Activity 21 per child

What to do:

1. Before starting this activity, divide one of the sheets of flipchart paper or one poster board into four squares, labeling each square with the name of an element, starting with earth. On the second sheet of paper or poster board make an oval in the center of the paper and print Sources of Information within the oval.

2. Start today's activity with the children by asking them to think about all the sources of information they used to find out more about their element. As children give their responses, use a mind map (see Activity 14 in the Appendix for examples) to create a graphic by categories to show the variety of sources used. These could include people, books, magazines, Web sites, movies, TV documentaries or other programs, and intuition (sixth sense). (You may need to briefly explain what intuition is, i.e., getting answers via mental images, thoughts, or feelings without knowing any concrete source/s of the information.)

3. Ask the children to share what facts they learned about their chosen or assigned elements. As the children give their answers, record the facts in the appropriate squares, or you can mind map their responses for each element in its square, if you prefer.

4. After recording all of the children's responses, ask them how they felt about doing their research. If you have time, you can ask them if they have a preferred way or ways to learn something new.

5. To help the children organize and remember what they learned about each of the four elements today, have them use the recording format provided under Activity 21 in the Appendix to write down the important things they learned from doing this activity.

Notes

Activity 66 *(3 in a Series of 6)*

Using the Natural Elements

Purpose of this activity: In day three of exploring the natural elements, the children think about, record, and discuss how they can use each of the four elements in their everyday lives, thus creating more appreciation for and understanding of them.

Timeframe: about 45 minutes total. You can adapt this activity to shorter time periods by covering just one, two, or three of the elements.

What you need: four, flipchart-size sheets of paper, pens or colored markers, and two sheets of drawing/writing paper for each child

What to do:

1. Explain to the children that today you are all going to explore how we use each of the elements and the benefits we derive from each. To begin this activity, ask each child to think about all the activities they did yesterday, from the time they got up until the time they went to bed, and write them down on one of their two sheets of paper.

2. Next, have the children take their second sheets of paper and fold them so they have four sections, one for each element. Have the children label each section, starting with water. Ask them to look through their activities on the first sheet to find all of the things they did that involved using water. Have them list these activities in the section labeled "water." Repeat this process for the remaining three elements. (Point out that the connection can be indirect, as long as the element was involved in the chain somewhere.)

3. Divide the group of children into four groups, one for each element. Give each group a large sheet of paper on which to list the activities they did that used the element assigned to that group.

4. When the groups of children have completed this task, have one person from each group post the group's list in a place in the room easily visible to everybody. Then, for each element, read (or have a child read) the list of activities included on the list. As you finish each element, ask the children to check their own lists and to raise their hands if they have something on their lists that is not included in the group list. Add these activities, and tell the children you will leave these lists up for the next two days so they can continue adding activities as they think of them. If the children are having difficulty coming up with ideas for each element, suggest that they look through magazines at home or talk to their parents, brothers, sisters, or friends, for additional ideas.

5. You can summarize this activity by saying something like the following: "Nature takes good care of us. The sun's fire provides light and heat energy for plants, animals, and people. Planet Earth provides soil and water to grow plants, which people and animals eat. We drink, bathe, and play in Earth's water. And, of course, we breathe the air that surrounds our planet." Ask the children if they would like to share other summarizing statements about how we benefit in our daily lives from the natural elements.

6. Conclude this activity by asking the children the question: "How can we show we care about our planet and appreciate the many benefits it gives us?" Encourage the children to think about this question so they can share their ideas later (on day six of this series).

Notes

Activity 67 *(4 in a Series of 6)*

Exploring Natural Elements Through Imagery, Symbolism, and Movement

Purpose of this activity: This activity helps children become more familiar with the four natural elements of water, air, fire, and earth through imagery, symbolism, and movement.

Timeframe: about 45 minutes. The length of this activity will depend on the size of your group and the age/s of the children.

What you need: comfortable places for the children to sit and space adequate for movement

What to do:

1. Tell the children that this activity has three parts, and each will help them further understand and relate to the four natural elements we share with planet Earth. The three parts involve imagery, symbolism, and movement.

2. Explain the concept of imagery as pictures (which can be in your mind or in physical form) and symbolism as simple pictures that represent particular things or ideas. For example, an image of camping might be a scene that includes trees, a tent, a campfire, a lake, and campers in outdoor clothing. On the other hand, a symbol for camping might be a simple picture of a tent or a campfire. The symbol would be the kind of picture you might see on a sign indicating that a particular area is for camping.

3. The imagery part of this activity involves imagining scenes that have to do with the four elements of water, earth, air, and fire. The symbolism part involves coming up with symbols to represent each element. The movement part entails thinking of and performing movements that represent the four elements. The movements are actually symbols in action. To come up with these symbols, the children can close their eyes for a few seconds, think of the element, and allow one or more images to appear in their minds. Have one or two children share the images they got and put the images to movement, or have volunteers put them to movement. An alternative is to first brainstorm ideas out loud.

4. Tell the children that they will be dividing into three groups, and each group will go to a different area of the room: the imagery area, the symbolism area, and the movement area. Those in the imagery area will be thinking of images, or scenes, that have to do with the four elements; those in the symbolism area will come up with symbols for the elements; and those in the movement area will think of and perform movements (or postures) that represent the elements. (Tell the movement group that they can come up with movements or postures and can use something related to the element, as earth/soil might be a challenge. For example, you might prompt them to come up with something like one of the following ideas for earth: lie on the floor to represent the earth under our feet; turn in place to represent planet Earth, which is partially made of soil; move as a plant growing out of the soil; or act as if shoveling dirt. Creativity is the name of the game!)

5. Let the children know that you will time them and give them two minutes to think about an element and four minutes to share their ideas with the others in the group—or, in the movement area, to act out movements for the element. They will do one element at a time. Then they will have two minutes to choose a spokesperson for the group, who will share one image/symbol/movement for each element with the larger group. (If there is time, they can share more.) The spokesperson should share ideas from the group and not just his or her own. The group can take part of the two minutes deciding which to share, if they like. Overall, the children will be in their groups for about 30 minutes. (You can vary the timing as you think advisable for your group.)

6. When each group has gone through all of the four elements, they will gather as a large group for the spokespeople to share the group ideas. The movement spokesperson will perform one movement that his/her group came up with for each element, or the movement group can perform the movements together. Have the children in the other groups guess what each movement represents, then if they can't guess, have the spokesperson explain it.

7. To bring this activity to a close, ask the children to voluntarily share what this experience was like for them and what new discoveries they made about each of the elements as a result of this experience.

Notes

Exploring Natural Elements Through Art

Purpose of this activity: This activity helps children become more familiar with the four natural elements of water, air, fire, and earth through art. It puts the children's imagery and symbolism from the fourth activity in this series into concrete form. Each element is represented by a particular medium, so you may choose the element/medium for the children to use, or divide this activity into four parts and use each medium on a different day to represent each of the four elements.

Timeframe: about 45 minutes for each of the four elements/media. The length of this activity will depend on the size of your group and the age/s of the children.

What you need: You can come up with your own ideas for media to represent the four elements, or use one or more of the following: watercolor paints for water; chalk (pastels) for earth; poster paint using the "dry-brush" method for air; and embossing (which uses a heat gun) for fire. You will need the following supplies for these media:

Watercolor: watercolor paints, brushes, and paper; paper towels
Poster paint: poster paints, brushes (stiffer than watercolor brushes), and paper; paper towels
Pastels: pastel chalks and appropriate drawing paper
Embossing: rubber stamp/s; embossing ink in a stamp pad and embossing powder; white cardstock paper; heat gun

What to do:

1.   Tell the children that they will be putting the images and symbols they came up with for the four elements into art forms. Explain which medium they will be using this time and why/how it represents its particular element (obvious with watercolors, but not so obvious with the others). They are to create artwork that relates to the images and symbols and perhaps even the movements they came up with for the particular element related to this medium. (E.g., if you are using watercolors, have them paint a picture that relates to water.)

2.   Explain how to use the medium of choice for the day. You may have to do a little research on your medium, or ask an art teacher to help. A few hints:

   • ***Watercolor (water):*** With watercolor paints, tell the children that the more water they mix with the paint, the lighter the color will be, which can work well when painting large areas such as skies or lakes or oceans. They need to be careful, however, not to use too much water, as the paint will take a long time to dry and will soak the paper too much. If they use just a little water, they can concentrate the color for outlines or darker, more solid colors. They can use the paper towels to blot the extra water off their brushes.

   • ***Poster paint dry-brush (air):*** In using the dry-brush method with poster paints, they will need to use just a little paint and should blot their brushes quite a bit on paper towels before they paint so they get a light, airy, feathery look in their paintings. (They needn't mix water with the paints.) The bristle marks of the somewhat stiff brush should show on the paper.

- ***Pastels (earth):*** Pastels are perhaps the easiest of these media to use. Choose a color and draw! (Their pictures can include more than brown soil. How about an earthworm or green plants, colorful flowers, or vegetables sticking up out of the soil? Remind the children of the images they generated in the previous activity.) Talk about the fact that soil and rocks are partly formed from decayed animals and plants (hence the fossils we find within rock). Real chalk is a type of limestone created from the shells of sea animals, so this medium could be considered to have connections with both earth and water. Commercial chalk is made from other materials, but virtually everything must be made from something that comes from or is somehow related to the earth.

- ***Embossing (fire):*** Embossing is perhaps the most involved of these media, but the results are fun and different. Caution must be taken with the heat gun, which should not be used by the children. Stamps come in different designs, and you can look for one that has fire or the sun or a candle on it to represent the fire element.

  The process involves pressing the stamp on the ink pad and stamping it on the cardstock, then sprinkling embossing powder over the stamped image. When heated with the heat gun, the design becomes slightly raised and hardens when it cools. You can get either colored ink or colored powder. Make sure to use some yellow, orange, and/or red for fire.

  You may want to use only one stamp and have the children take turns at the embossing table, where you supervise. The other children can draw fire pictures or symbols with crayons and markers while they wait their turns.

3. When the children have completed their artwork, get together as a group and have them share what they have done. How do their pictures reflect the chosen element? What insights did they gain from this activity?

Notes

Activity 69 *(6 in a Series of 6)*

Exploring Natural Elements: Interdependence and Caring

Purpose of this activity: This activity celebrates and honors the four natural elements of air, water, earth, and fire that we and planet Earth share by recognizing our interdependence and finding ways that we can care for and protect our environment. By doing so, we also show we care about ourselves, and we open ourselves to more balance in our lives.

Timeframe: about 30 minutes

What you need: chalkboard and chalk or flipchart and markers; paper and writing utensils for one person (the recorder) in each group, if you divide the children into groups

What to do:

1. To begin this activity, share the following statements with the children:

    ### Air
    > We breathe in oxygen from the air for life and growth, and we breathe out carbon dioxide.
    > Plants and trees take in carbon dioxide, and they give back oxygen to us.
    > We are air.

    ### Water
    > Our bodies are about 70 percent water, which exists in our every cell.
    > Planet Earth is about 74 percent water, and it gives us water to drink.
    > We are water.

    ### Fire
    > Light and warmth are vital to our lives.
    > Our bodies need energy to live, work, and play.
    > The sun gives light and heat energy to us and to the plants we eat.
    > We are fire.

    ### Earth
    > Planet Earth is our home. It provides the soil for plants to grow that animals eat.
    > Plants and animals give us food to build and strengthen our bodies.
    > We are earth.

    Note: If you have not already clarified this for the children, explain that Earth with a capital *E* refers to the planet, whereas earth with a lowercase *e* refers to the soil of planet Earth.

2. After reading the above statements, ask the children to share any additional thoughts. Then conclude this part of the activity by asking: "If we are air, water, fire, and earth, and planet Earth is air, water, fire, and earth, what things can we do to help and protect the planet?" Point out that by helping and

protecting planet Earth, we are also taking care of ourselves and ensuring our very survival. We also are providing all living things with a better place in which to live, work, and play.

3. Present the idea of the three Rs for taking care of planet Earth: Recycle; Reuse; Reduce. Write these three words on the board or flipchart. You may need to explain these terms to younger children and give them some examples of each. You also may want to focus on just these three ways of helping save and protect planet Earth.

4. After you have discussed the three Rs, if you have older children, divide them into groups of four or five, and ask them to brainstorm additional ways they can care for and protect our planet. What other things are they already doing to help? What additional actions can they take? Depending on the age group, you also might have them brainstorm ways that industries, governments, and other organizations can help. Give the children about 10 minutes to meet in their groups. Have a volunteer in each group record the group's ideas.

5. At the end of the 10 minutes, ask the groups to stop the brainstorming and take a few minutes to think about all of the ideas given. Have each person choose one idea on which he or she will take action and share it with their group members. If you have time, you can have each child share his or her action with the whole group of children. When sharing is completed, encourage the children also to share their action ideas with their families and to ask other family members to take the same or another action to help planet Earth.

6. To extend this activity and make it an ongoing project, combine the groups' lists of the actions the children are already taking and the new ones they added. Post this master list in a convenient place, and encourage the children to keeping adding to it.

    You might make copies of the master list so each child can take one home to encourage their parents, siblings, and other adults they know to get involved in taking positive actions to care for our planet. Depending on what time of year you do these activities, you could have a celebration of all the children accomplished to save and protect planet Earth on Earth Day, which occurs in March.

    Note: For ideas of actions children can take, refer to *The Complete Guide to Service Learning* (Chapter 8, The Environment), listed in the Resource section at the back of this book.

"Our survival depends on remembering who we are. We are the Earth—part of the air, water, soil, and energy of the world; beings with love in our hearts, life in our souls, and a kingdom of kin at our doorstep. It is up to us to protect those things so that they will be around for many generations to come."

David Suzuki, *You Are the Earth*, p.109

Notes

Activity 70

Animals as Teachers

Purpose of this activity: We have many teachers in our lives and many sources of learning. The purpose of this activity is to explore the idea of animals as teachers and what we do and can learn from animals. As learning is one of the purposes of life, this type of activity can help enhance meaning in a child's life as well as develop understanding of other creatures.

Timeframe: 15-45 minutes, depending upon the age group and how much you wish to extend this activity

What you need: pictures the children bring in, magazines containing animal pictures, and paper and drawing utensils if you do the last parts of this activity

What to do:

1. A few days before you do this activity with the children, ask them to look for a picture or pictures of their favorite animal or animals. Encourage them to bring photographs they, themselves, or their families have taken. If they don't have photographs, ask them to look in magazines or books they have at home for pictures of their favorite animals and to bring in the books or magazine pictures. The day before you do this activity, remind the children to come with their pictures the next day. (Families could do this activity at home.)

2. Before you start this activity, check to see if each child has a photograph or picture of his/her favorite animal. If not, allow a few minutes for the children who don't have a picture to find one in magazines you supply.

3. To start this activity, have all the children join you in a circle or other appropriate formation with their pictures of their favorite animals. Then, have everyone hold up their pictures in front of them (if in a circle) so others can see the animals chosen. Note the similarities and differences in their choices of animals.

4. Next, have everyone whose favorite animal is a pet give the name of the pet and tell how he or she got the pet. Then, one at a time, have the other children hold up their pictures and tell the others the reasons the animals they chose are favorites.

5. When all the children have finished sharing, ask them to think about and tell the others what they have learned from being with and observing their respective animals and/or from what they know about the qualities and habits of their favorite animals. Summarize these comments, and encourage the children to continue to observe animals and discover what each animal can teach us. You may stop the activity at this point, or go on to #6.

6. Have the children return to their places, and give them drawing paper and drawing utensils. Ask them each to draw one of their favorite animals (if they chose more than one) in the setting they are usually in with this animal or the setting that represents the animal's natural habitat.

7. After they have completed their drawings, have the children list as many things as possible that they have learned from their pets and/or favorite animals.

8. You may want to have each child share what they have drawn and written and/or post all the papers in the room. If you like, refer back to the children's drawings and comments at a later date to ask what new things they have learned from animals. Remind the children that animals can be teachers for human beings, just as human beings can be teachers for animals. You might extend this concept to the interconnectedness between human beings and animals. (See Activity 42 for how people and animals express emotions.)

Note: A possible introduction or follow-up to this activity would be to take a field trip to a local zoo and observe various animals as a stimulus for the activity or to discover more ways in which animals teach us.

Notes

Activity 71

Experiencing Music Inspired by Nature

Purpose of this activity: Throughout history, nature has been an inspiration for people to: compose music; create forms of dance and exercise; capture nature's colors, patterns, and forms on canvas; write poetry and prose; design buildings that reflect natural beauty and harmony; and mirror nature's magnificence in a myriad of other ways. The purpose of this activity is to give children the opportunity to experience music inspired by the seasons of nature by listening and responding to Vivaldi's *Four Seasons*.

Timeframe: 30-45 minutes, depending on which parts of the activity you choose to do on the same day

What you need: a recording of Vivaldi's *Four Seasons,* an audio player, writing/drawing utensils, paper, and an appropriate space in which to move

What to do:

1. Before introducing this activity to the children, select one or more excerpts from one of Vivaldi's *Four Seasons*. Choose music you like, that has vivid imagery associated with it, and, if you like, that coincides with the season in which you are doing this activity.

2. Instruct the children to find a comfortable place to sit so they can put their full attention on listening to some music you will be playing for them that is meant to musically portray one of the seasons of nature: either spring, summer, autumn, or winter. They are to close their eyes to shut out visual distractions so they can more easily tune in to the music and see if they can tell what season the music is portraying. Point out that they might get pictures in their minds, feelings, or just a sense of what season it is as they listen to it. Explain that when the music ends, you will ask for volunteers to guess the season.

3. Play the excerpt from Vivaldi's *Four Seasons* that you have chosen. The length of time you have the children listen will depend on the age/s of the children. For example, for very young children, each segment would be no more than two to three minutes.

4. When you stop the music, ask the children to open their eyes. Allow them a few moments to recall the images, feelings, and thoughts they had when they were listening to the music. Have the children share what they pictured and felt. What season do they think the music represents? Ask if anyone recognized the music and/or the composer of the music they just heard. Share a few facts with the children about Vivaldi and how nature's seasons inspired him to compose *Four Seasons*. Once they know for sure which season you played, you might want to play it again, so perhaps they can now see in their minds what the composer saw in his mind as he composed the piece.

5. Next, playing the same excerpt of music, have the children stand about an arm's length away from other children. Tell them that this time they listen to the music they are to try to capture the feeling and imagery of the music through movement. Encourage them to listen to the music and express through body postures and movement what the music is "saying" to them.

Note: Generally children of all ages are more free to express images, feelings, and thoughts through movement if you move with them. For some children, you may need to demonstrate possibilities.

6. After about three minutes of movement (or longer, if you wish, for older children), have the children stop and join you in a circle. Encourage them to share their thoughts, feelings, and any new insights about the music that they were able to access through movement.

7. Point out that mental imagery and movement are two ways we can "feel" and "see" music. Dancing, for example, is a means of expressing how music feels to us. Also, music can inspire us to write or illustrate in pictures and symbols what the music makes us feel and see.

   Ask the children to choose one of the following options:

   - Write a poem about some aspect of nature based on thoughts and feelings that were inspired by listening to the excerpt from Vivaldi's *Four Seasons*.

   - Write a few paragraphs that express how nature may have inspired Vivaldi to compose this music.

   - Write a few paragraphs about how nature has inspired your own thoughts, feelings, and/or actions.

   - Represent the imagery inspired by the music by creating a symbol or picture on paper using the colors that reflect your thoughts and feelings.

   Note: Have the music playing in the background while children do this task. If you prefer, #7 could be a follow-up activity for another day. For this part, you can encourage the children to allow their inner feelings and thoughts to direct their writing and drawing, or you can introduce this section by reading a poem reflective of the music, and/or you can have the children recall what words came to mind while listening to the music. Record the children's responses, pointing out that they can use these words and ideas to inspire their writing and drawing.

8. On completion of #7, have the children voluntarily share their poems, writings, or pictures with the rest of the children.

9. This activity can be an on-going project, in which you play excerpts from the other seasons and introduce additional music with strong images, such as Handel's *Water Music,* Tchaikovsky's "Waltz of the Flowers" from *The Nutcracker,* or Debussy's *La Mer* (The Sea).

Notes

Activity 72

Taking a Moment to Feel Love

Purpose of this activity: To love and be loved is a basic human need. The purpose of this activity is to have children learn how to connect with this love on a regular basis.

Timeframe: five minutes or less

What you need: a comfortable space in which to sit or stand

What to do:

1. Ask the children to stop whatever they are doing in order to take a few minutes to experience the love we have for others and the love others have for us.

2. When the children are seated or standing comfortably, have them put their right hands over their left hands, place both of their hands over the heart area, and then close their eyes.

3. Encourage the children to think of someone they love very much. Have the children make mental pictures of their people (or animals) and surround them with pink light. Then, have the children feel the love they have for these people or animals in their hearts.

4. Next, have the children (still with eyes closed and hands on hearts) think of people who love them. Have the children make mental pictures of these people (or animals) and feel love coming into their hearts from these people or animals. Again, they might want to visualize the love as pink light, which makes it more tangible.

5. Ask children to quietly open their eyes and feel the love from everyone around them.

6. Encourage the children to do this on their own first thing in the morning when they wake up, several times throughout the day, and just before they go to sleep at night.

7. An extension of this activity is to do it with people the children don't like and surround those people with pink light. Ask the children to try to think of something they like about these people, even if it's the color of someone's shirt or the style of someone's hair. As difficult as it may be to do this activity with people they don't like, it has resulted in many positive changes in relationships. One shy boy who was being bullied at school and didn't even want to go to school began mentally surrounding his bullies in pink light for a few moments every day. Soon they stopped their bullying, and the boy no longer feared going to school. In fact, he became president of his class.

Notes

Activity 73

Tuning in to Your Talents

Purpose of this activity: Children, as well as people in general, feel more balanced and fulfilled when they are aware of and use their innate talents. Once they tune in to what they are naturally good at doing, they can consciously develop skills that enhance these gifts. Then, they can use them most effectively in the world and be of service to others. This service gives them a sense of worth and connectedness. Tuning in to your talents is a way of nourishing your spirit.

Timeframe: about 10 minutes (and can be extended with a Talent Show, if you like)

What you need: no materials needed

What to do:

1. Introduce this activity by explaining the purpose of tuning in to your talents, rewording the purpose above to fit your age group. Tell them that, today, they are going to pretend they are tuning in to a TV show about their lives and what they are good at and love to do. They will be imagining this show in their minds. To do this, they need to be quiet and still and just have fun daydreaming about it. Tell them you will guide them in this adventure.

2. Have the children sit comfortably, take a few slow, deep breaths from their bellies, and close their eyes to reduce distractions. (If any children are uncomfortable closing their eyes, have them look at a spot on the floor and let their eyes go into "soft focus," as they do when they are daydreaming.)

3. Then, guide the children through the following experience of imaging, using the script below and pacing your words so the children have time to imagine the scenes:

    Picture yourself on a big-screen TV. You are doing something you love to do and you are good at doing. Maybe it is something you are doing with your hands or your body. Maybe it is something you are using your mind to do. You might be with other people. If so, what are you doing with them? How is your caring heart involved? Where are you, and what is around you? How do you feel about doing something you love to do and that you do well? Imagine that feeling throughout your body. Now wave goodbye to your TV audience, and slowly begin to bring your mind back to this room. When you are ready, open your eyes.

4. Ask for volunteers to share what the experience was like for them and what they saw themselves doing. Did they create something? Did they sing? Were they good at some kind of movement, such as dancing, or game, such as hockey? Or were they good at things such as doing puzzles or putting together models? Did they especially like being around people or doing something alone? Encourage each child to zero in on his or her strengths and talents.

5. Consider doing this activity periodically throughout the year. Ask the children if their interests have changed. What have they been doing to develop their talents and skills?

6. You may want to extend this activity by having a Talent Show, if it seems appropriate for your group. Just preparing for the show can utilize some talents. Who will help with the organizing?

Who will design and make the backdrop and/or props? Who will announce the performers? If you allow it to be just a fun event instead of a contest, more children may feel free to participate.

Notes

Activity 74

What a Joke!

Purpose of this activity: The main purpose of this activity is to have fun and laugh! In doing so, we actually help to balance and heal our bodies. In addition, the classroom (or family) that laughs together, is likely to get along better.

Timeframe: about 10-15 minutes (and can be repeated as often as you like)

What you need: joke books appropriate for your age group and small sticky-note pads

What to do:

1. Tell the children you'd like to take a little time to have fun and laugh. Explain that laughter can help heal what ails you and lift everyone's spirits.

2. Divide the group into several smaller groups of three, four, or five. Pass out the joke books and sticky-note pads so that every group has one of each.

   (**Note:** For younger children, you may want to read jokes to them and then ask which they liked the best. You might also ask if the children know jokes they want to share with the others and/or encourage them to bring jokes from home.)

3. Tell the groups that for the next eight or so minutes they are to take turns reading the jokes out loud to each other from the books they have been given. They can feel free to laugh! Each group is to mark with sticky notes the jokes the group likes the best, then when the time is up, they are to decide on one joke to share with the group as a whole.

4. Ready, set, LAUGH!

Notes

Activity 75

Courage and Caring

Purpose of this activity: Courage and caring are gifts of the spirit, and this activity is meant to heighten the children's awareness of these qualities and to encourage the expression of them in the children's daily lives.

Timeframe: for older children, about 45 minutes for the first session and about 15-20 minutes for the second session (sharing their reports), depending on the number of children; for younger children, 20-30 minutes

What you need: paper and writing utensils for older children; a short book on a famous person who has demonstrated courage and caring to read to younger children

What to do:

1. Begin this activity by telling the children that today you will all be talking about courage and caring. Ask the children what they think it means to have courage and what it means to be caring.

   Ask for volunteers to give the names of people they know or have heard of who have expressed both these qualities in their lives, and have the children explain how these people have shown courage and caring.

   Point out that sometimes people give up something in their own lives to demonstrate courage or caring. Sometimes they choose courage in the face of misfortune or difficulty when they could have caved in. Sometimes they spend a lot of their own time and effort caring and doing something about a cause or helping others. However, also point out that we don't have to be great heroes. We can show courage and caring in our own ways, and often our little acts of kindness will have big effects on others. Ask the children how they think our courage and caring can also help *us*.

2. Give the (older) children paper and writing utensils and tell them you would like them to write about how they show courage and caring in their own lives as well as how they might extend their courage and caring in new ways. Give them about 10 minutes to think and write.

3. Then, gather in a group again, and ask for volunteers to share what they've written.

4. After they have shared, tell the children you would like them to research a famous person who is known for his or her courage and caring. Give each child a list of such people, which might include Mother Teresa, Gandhi, Martin Luther King Jr., Rosa Parks, and Christopher Reeves. (The children may have mentioned one or more of these people in their discussion.) Ask each child to choose one person to research. It's okay if some share the same people. Tell them they can use books, the Internet, or any other resource they can find for their research. They can ask the librarian or their parents to help them. You would like them to read about their people and find out how they showed courage and caring and write a paragraph or two about them. Give the children an appropriate number of days to do this.

Note: With younger children, you can talk about one famous person and perhaps read a short book to them about the person. You may want to extend this activity and discuss a different person every week for as long as you wish.

5.   When the children have finished their research projects, ask them to share what they learned about the people they chose, making sure to cover all the different people they researched.

6.   Ask the children what they have learned about courage and caring and if they can see even more ways to express these qualities in their lives. Suggest that they choose one of their insights and put it into action.

"At the center of the Universe is a loving heart that continues to beat and that wants the best for every person. Anything that we can do to help foster the intellect and spirit and emotional growth of our fellow human beings, that is our job. Those of us who have this particular vision must continue against all odds. Life is for service."

Fred Rogers (a.k.a., "Mister Rogers") 1928-2003

Notes

Appendix

Appendix Activity 1

Balance and Me

Complete these sentences about balance as they relate to your life.

I think balance means _____

_____

When my body is balanced, I _____

_____

When my mind is balanced, I _____

_____

When my emotions (feelings) are balanced, I _____

_____

When I'm out of balance, my body _____

_____

When I'm out of balance, my mind _____

_____

When I'm out of balance, my emotions _____

_____

I get out of balance when _____

_____

I can help myself be more balanced by _____

_____

_____

_____

Appendix Activity 2

The Wheel of Balance

Balance within an individual depends on maintaining harmony within and between mental, physical, and emotional/social functions. Elizabeth Kubler-Ross, M.D., adds a fourth dimension —that of spirituality. She refers to these four human functions as the "four quadrants" that make up a whole individual. To achieve a state of inner balance and to realize one's full capabilities, all four quadrants need to be nurtured and expressed. This wholeness concept of balance is portrayed below as a wheel.

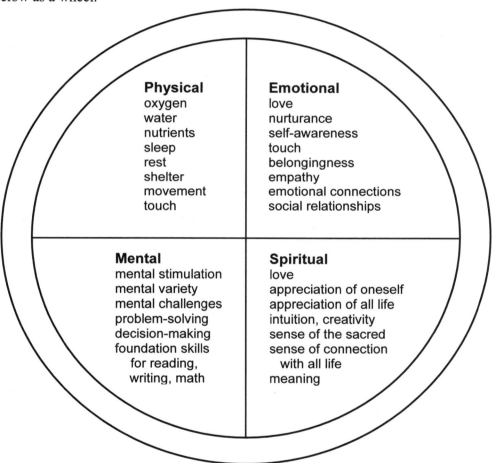

Physical
oxygen
water
nutrients
sleep
rest
shelter
movement
touch

Emotional
love
nurturance
self-awareness
touch
belongingness
empathy
emotional connections
social relationships

Mental
mental stimulation
mental variety
mental challenges
problem-solving
decision-making
foundation skills
 for reading,
 writing, math

Spiritual
love
appreciation of oneself
appreciation of all life
intuition, creativity
sense of the sacred
sense of connection
 with all life
meaning

The Wheel of Balance Model

On the next page is a blank wheel that you can copy for the children to fill in with their own ideas for each quadrant. Make one copy for each child to illustrate with pictures, and make a second copy for each child who can write to list what he or she is doing and can do further to take care of each quadrant of life.

The Wheel of Balance

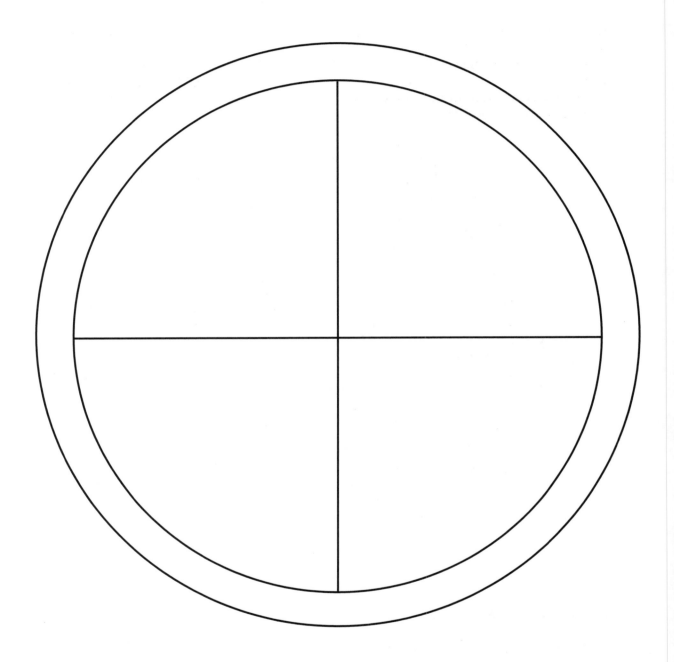

Appendix Activity 3

Self-Care of My Body

Taking care of my body means that I:

- drink an adequate amount of good quality water (8-12 glasses) every day

- breath as deeply as possible from the lower abdomen and stop to take deep breaths throughout the day to bring extra oxygen into my body, brain, and heart

- eat three balanced meals every day that include protein, complex carbohydrates, "good" fats, and a variety of food

- do a variety of exercises and movements several times a day

- rest when I get tired

- get an adequate amount and quality of sleep for my age every night

Specific self-care activities (based on letters in the word *balance*) that I can do to help keep my body in balance include:

B: biking, batting a ball, _____

A: aerobic activity,* such as jumping on a trampoline, _____

L: lap swimming, _____

A: _____

N: napping when tired, nutrients for the body, _____

C: cardiovascular activity,** such as running, _____

E: eating balanced meals and snacks, _____

In the space below, continue listing or drawing symbols of other ways you can help your body so you can feel good physically and have the energy to do the activities you need to do. You do not need to use the letters in the word *balance* in adding to this list.

---

*aerobic activity: activity that causes the body to use more oxygen (helping body processes)
**cardiovascular activity: activity that causes a temporary increase in heartrate (exercising the heart and blood vessels)

Appendix Activity 4

Self-Care of My Heart

Taking care of my heart means that I:

- receive and feel love every day from at least one person through a hug, words of love, a loving smile, or some other way of showing love

- give an expression of love to someone every day

- spend time with a friend or friends every day to talk or do something together

- feel a sense of belonging when I am with my family and friends

- have some alone time every day to calm my emotions

Specific self-care activities (based on the letters in the word *balance*) that I can do to help keep my heart in balance include:

B: bond with people close to me, _____

A: appreciate myself and others, _____

L: love myself and others, _____

A: _____

N: nurture myself and others, _____

C: care about myself and others, call a friend, _____

E: empathize* with others, enjoy others, _____

In the space below, continue listing or drawing symbols of other ways in which you can help keep your heart balanced to support feeling good about yourself, feeling good about being with others, and experiencing a sense of belonging. You do not need to use the letters in the word *balance* in adding to this list.

*empathize:** to understand how others feel

142

Appendix Activity 5

Self-Care of My Mind

Taking care of my mind means that I:

- exercise my five senses of seeing, hearing, tasting, smelling, and touching every day by engaging in a variety of activities to help bring new information into my brain and mind

- seek out activities that challenge my mind to think in new and creative ways every day

- practice problem-solving and decision-making in everyday situations

- use a variety of ways to learn, such as reading books, talking to other people, watching videos and DVDs, doing hands-on activities, listening to music, watching a sunset …

- take in the air, water, and nutrients that are needed daily to help my brain perform its thinking functions

Specific self-care activities (based on the letters in the word *balance*) that I can do to help keep my mind in balance include:

B: brainstorm new ideas and thoughts, breathe deeply, _____

A: actively be involved in learning, _____

L: learn a new skill, _____

A: _____

N: nurture* my body, heart, and spirit, _____

C: challenge what I believe with new ideas, _____

E: elicit** thoughts and ideas from others, experience new activities, _____

In the space below, continue listing or drawing symbols of other ways you can help your mind be balanced so you can enjoy learning and perform to your highest ability. You do not need to use the letters in the word *balance* in adding to this list.

---

*nurture: pay attention to, take care of, encourage, make stronger
**elicit: bring out

Appendix Activity 6

Self-Care of My Spirit

Taking care of my spirit means that I:

- take time to be alone to better "tune in" to my inner world of hopes, dreams, passions, and peace

- find meaning and joy in life

- follow my dreams and use my talents

- spend time in nature to experience and appreciate the interconnectedness of all life

- look for and appreciate the beauty and goodness in myself, others, and my surroundings

- nurture* my sense of wonder and respect for the mysteries of the universe

- care about other people and lifeforms

- seek out and experience being in a sacred space such as a church, synagogue, mosque, or other place of worship, and/or find a sense of the sacred by being in nature

Specific self-care activities (based on the letters in the word *balance*) that I can do to nurture my spirit in order to bring more balance into my life include:

B: be still, balance doing with being, _____

A: attend a sacred ceremony or event, appreciate all forms of life, _____

L: listen to sacred and inspiring music, listen to my inner voice of knowing, _____

A: _____

N: note the beauty in myself, others, and my environment, _____

C: create a story, a poem, or art expressing beauty, peace, joy, or love, _____

E: engage in activities that help others or the planet, _____

In the space below, continue listing or drawing symbols of ways you can nourish your spirit and bring more balance into your life. You do not need to use the letters in the word *balance* when you add to this list.

*****nurture:** pay attention to, encourage, and make stronger

Appendix Activity 7

Resources for Cooperative Learning About Balance

This first page is for your reference. The second page includes a rating form (two on the page) that can be copied for the children to rate themselves on their behavior and set goals for improvement.

Behaviors Often Associated with Children in a Balanced State

- appear to be happy, smile, laugh, enjoy what they are doing
- get along well with others
- look healthy and act in a way to indicate their bodies are being nurtured and cared for
- engage in a variety of tasks
- are helpful to others
- receive affection and praise comfortably
- show affection towards others
- have positive outlooks on life
- set goals and generally achieve them
- show empathy and care about others
- demonstrate a sense of confidence

Add to this list as you and the children identify other behaviors appropriate for your age group that are associated with being in a state of balance.

Behaviors Often Associated with Children Who Are Out of Balance

- appear sad, get easily discouraged, get mad easily
- bully or are aggressive towards others
- have frequent colds, headaches, and/or stomachaches
- get tired easily
- often complain about being bored
- are fearful of new situations
- avoid others
- worry a lot
- display negative attitudes
- have trouble sleeping
- have difficulty making and keeping friends
- see the world as a hostile place
- blame others for the consequences of their own actions
- often have feelings of hopelessness

Add to this list as you and the children identify other behaviors appropriate for your age group that are associated with being in a state of imbalance.

"HELPING MYSELF IMPROVE" FORM

For_____   Date:_____

Circle the rating that fits for you today:

Today I did   well   okay   not so well   on **listening**

Today I did   well   okay   not so well   in **taking turns**

Today I did   well   okay   not so well   in **cooperating with others**

Today I did   well   okay   not so well   in **participating in my group**

Next time we meet in groups my goal is to: _____

_____

_____

_____

- -

"HELPING MYSELF IMPROVE" FORM

For_____   Date:_____

Circle the rating that fits for you today:

Today I did   well   okay   not so well   on **listening**

Today I did   well   okay   not so well   in **taking turns**

Today I did   well   okay   not so well   in **cooperating with others**

Today I did   well   okay   not so well   in **participating in my group**

Next time we meet in groups my goal is to: _____

_____

_____

_____

Appendix Activity 8

Food Colors Bar Graph

Foods have many colors. Which color is found the most in foods you know? Find out by making a Food Colors Bar Graph!

Directions: Create your bars on the graph started below. Colors are listed along the bottom, and numbers up the side. Write the names of foods under their colors, and for each food, color a box that color above the color name. For example, "red" might have "strawberry" written under it and a red square colored in above it. Other guidelines include:

- For white food, use black and trace the outline of a square above "white."

- Brown means anything from tan to dark brown.

- If foods come in more than one color, you can list them under all their colors, but only under the colors of the parts we eat. Don't count parts we don't eat.

- List single foods and not foods that have more than one ingredient, such as pizza.

12							
11							
10							
9							
8							
7							
6							
5							
4							
3							
2							
1							
	RED	*YELLOW*	*BLUE*	*GREEN*	*ORANGE*	*PURPLE*	*WHITE*

Appendix Activity 9

Food-O! Game

How to Play Food-O!

The object of the game is to see who can be the first to fill one row of boxes on the game board with cards. A row may be filled vertically, horizontally, or diagonally, as in the games tic-tac-toe and bingo.

When a square is called out (such as B3) and a plant part given (such as root), find a card in your pile with a food in that category and put it on that square. Whoever completes a row first wins. If all the squares are called and no one has completed a row, whoever has the most cards in a row wins. There may be more than one winner.

The caller of the squares will let you know if you can use a category list to determine the categories of the foods on your cards.

Food-O! Game Board

	A	B	C	D
1				
2				
3				
4				

Food-O! Game Cards

Picture version

watermelon	tomato	strawberry	pineapple
green bean	corn	peas	rice
artichoke	broccoli	cauliflower	nasturtium
peanut	almond	walnut	coconut

(Across)
Row 1: fruits
Row 2: seeds
Row 3: flowers (three florets, or immature flower heads, and one edible flower.)
Row 4: nuts

Food-O! Game Cards

Picture version

carrot	beet	potato	yam
celery	asparagus	rhubarb	kohlrabi
cabbage	leaf lettuce	spinach	parsley
apple	banana	orange	pear

(Across)
Row 1: roots
Row 2: stems (Kohlrabi is often mistaken for a root vegetable, but it is actually a stem.)
Row 3: leaves
Row 4: more fruits

Food-O! Game Board

	A	B	C	D	E	F
1						
2						
3						
4						
5						
6						

Food-O! Game Cards

beet	cabbage	cranberry	plum	peanut
carrot	endive	cucumber	raspberry	pecan
parsnip	lettuce	kumquat	strawberry	walnut
potato	parsley	currant	tomato	bean
radish	spinach	eggplant	watermelon	corn
rutabaga	dandelion	mango	artichoke	oats
turnip	greens	nectarine	broccoli	pea
yam	apple	orange	cauliflower	pine nut
asparagus	avocado	papaya	almond	quinoa
celery	blackberry	peach	coconut	rice
kohlrabi	blueberry	pear	filbert	soybean
rhubarb	cantaloupe	pineapple	macadamia	wheat

CATEGORIES OF FOODS FROM PLANTS

Roots	Fruit	Flower Buds (Florets)
beet	apple	artichoke
carrot	avocado	broccoli
parsnip	blackberry	cauliflower
potato	blueberry	
radish	cantaloupe	Nuts
rutabaga	cranberry	almond
turnip	cucumber	coconut
yam	kumquat	filbert
	currant	macadamia
Stems	eggplant	peanut
asparagus	mango	pecan
celery	nectarine	walnut
kohlrabi	orange	
rhubarb	papaya	Seeds
	peach	bean
Leaves	pear	corn
cabbage	pineapple	oats
endive	plum	pea
lettuce	raspberry	pine nut
parsley	strawberry	quinoa (keenwah)
spinach	tomato	rice
dandelion greens	watermelon	soybean
		wheat

Appendix Activity 10

"What's for Breakfast?" Chart

Using the chart below, record what you eat for breakfast each day for five days. Then, notice how you feel the rest of the morning. Rate how your body feels, how sharp your mind is, and how balanced your emotions (feelings) are after each breakfast.

Try to eat a balanced breakfast each day by including: whole grain cereals and breads; proteins such as meat, eggs, cheese, and peanut butter; a fruit or vegetable; and milk or yogurt. For example, you might choose to have a slice or two of whole grain bread with peanut butter and banana slices on it along with a glass of milk or some yogurt. Have fun, and be creative with your choices!

Directions:

Under each day's column, list what you ate for breakfast that day. You may want to do this when you finish eating your breakfast, or you may want to plan your breakfast the night before and list the foods you are going to eat the next morning. This will give you a head start towards a balanced breakfast.

WHAT I HAD FOR BREAKFAST, DAYS 1-5

Day 1	Day 2	Day 3	Day 4	Day 5

During each morning, pay attention to how your body feels (energetic, tired, restless, relaxed...), how well you can think and stick to the tasks you need to do, and what your feelings are like while doing your tasks and being with others.

At noontime, rate your body, mind, and emotions. Give yourself a + if most of the morning was good for you in an area, a ~ if it was okay, and a − if, for example, your body was tired, your concentration and thinking were fuzzy, and/or you had feelings of frustration, sadness, discouragement, or similar feelings during your morning activities.

BREAKFAST'S EFFECTS

Days	Body	Mind	Emotions
1			
2			
3			
4			
5			

When you have finished the fifth day, complete the following sentences:

Looking at what I ate for breakfast and how my morning went, I noticed that …

Based on what I noticed these past five mornings, I need to continue …

Based on what I noticed these past five mornings, I need to change …

Note for Families: A good reference for nutrition is *The Family Nutrition Book: Everything You Need to Know About Feeding Your Children—from Birth Through Adolescence* by William Sears, M.D., and Martha Sears, R.N. Boston: Little, Brown and Company, 1999.

Appendix Activity 11

Creating a Positive Learning Experience

When you are about to do a new learning task:

1. Think of a time you felt good about doing or learning something. Close your eyes and picture that time in your mind.

    What were you doing?
    How did you feel about yourself?
    How did you feel about what you were doing?
    How did your body feel?
    Where were you, and what was the space around you like?

2. Keep this good feeling of success in your mind, and relax your body by taking three or four deep breaths from your belly.

3. Say to yourself one or more of the following statements, or write your own below:

    I can do this work.
    I can think clearly.
    I can be successful in doing this task.
    I feel good about myself as a learner.
    I remember what I am learning.
    It's okay to make mistakes while I'm learning. I learn from my mistakes.
    Learning gets easier and easier for me as I practice.

    Write your own positive statements about your specific task and your abilities:

    _____

    _____

    _____

    _____

4. Breathe deeply, relax, and enjoy learning.

GOOD JOB!

Appendix Activity 12

Five-Minute Mind Teaser

Cross out six letters so that the name of a common fruit is left.

S B I A X L N E A T N T E R A S

Appendix Activity 13

Guidelines for Brainstorming

The purpose of brainstorming is to be creative and unlimited in coming up with as many ideas as possible on a particular topic or for a specific purpose without judging the ideas, even though they may seem far-fetched—and to have fun in the process.

Steps in the Brainstorming Process

1. Following is one way to do brainstorming.

    - Have everyone sit in a circle or around a table, and go in order around the circle or table, with each person offering an idea—or passing if he or she does not have an idea to offer at the time.

    - Let the ideas flow freely, without thinking too much about them before saying them.

    - Have someone record the ideas as they are given.

    - Build on other people's ideas, if you like, by listening carefully and adding to what they say.

    - Do not interrupt the flow of ideas by asking questions, making statements, or making judgments about whether or not an idea will work.

    - Have a positive attitude that every idea given could be a possibility.

    - Allow pauses, as they give time for people to think of more ideas.

    - Stop the brainstorming process when no one can come up with any more ideas or you have run out of time.

2. Have everyone look at all the ideas recorded. Have someone read them aloud, or have everyone read them together.

3. Pick out the most useful ideas for your purpose either by a show of hands or by having people write down the ones they like the best and choosing the most popular ones.

4. Try one or more of these chosen ideas for your problem or situation, and keep the other ideas for a future time when they might be needed.

Appendix Activity 14

Mind Maps

MIND MAP OF AN OBJECT

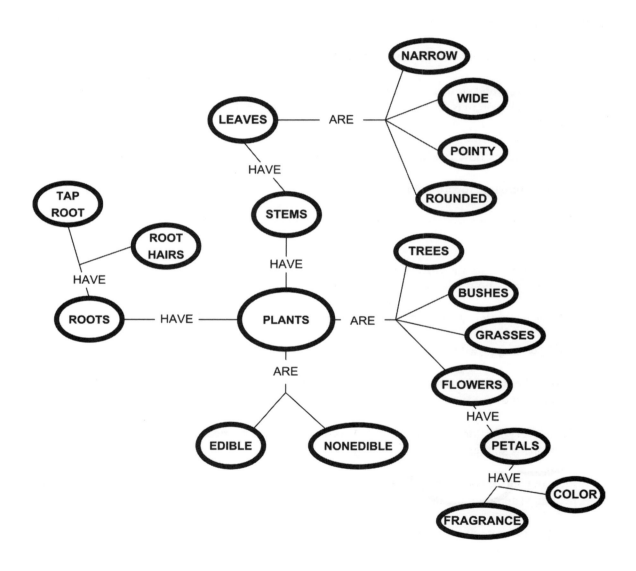

Mind Maps

MIND MAP OF A CONCEPT

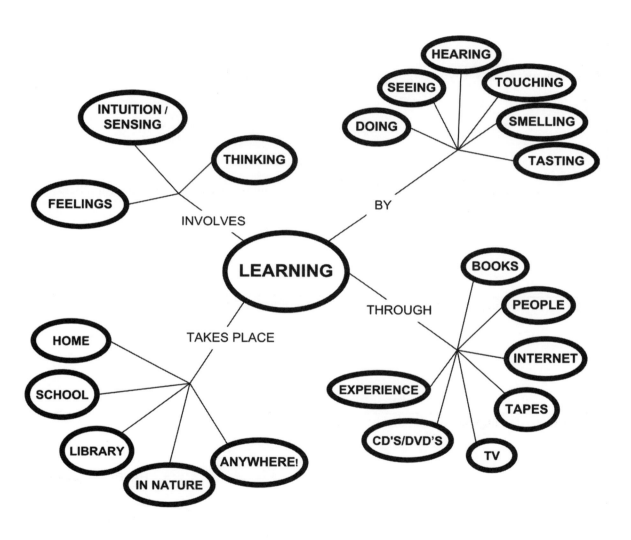

Appendix Activity 15

"My Feelings Are Important" Chart

List as many feelings as you can that help you to have positive and peaceful thoughts and actions:
List as many feelings as you can that help give you confidence in yourself:
List as many feelings as you can that help you feel you belong and can get along with others:
List as many feelings as you can that help you to learn new things:
List as many feelings as you can that help you have fun:

List as many feelings as you can that are hurtful to you, that get in the way of having positive feelings and thoughts, and that make it difficult for you to learn:

When you have finished this list of negative feelings, take a red or black marker and draw an X through each of these words. Then tear up this page and throw it in a wastebasket to show that you no longer wish to be bothered by these feelings.

Appendix Activity 16

Tapping Game Guide

The Tapping Game involves simply tapping on certain spots on your head and upper body to release blocked energy while saying what the problem is and saying good things about yourself (see below). It can help you feel better. Here's what you do:

Determine the problem. For example, "I'm restless and I can't focus on my work."

Rate how bad the problem is from 0 (no problem) to 10 (really, really bad or strong).

If the problem is really, really bad (or, in this case, you're really, really restless), it's a 10, and if there's no problem (you're perfectly calm and focused), it's a 0.

Note: The goal of the game is to get yourself down to 0.

Do the "kickoff."

Find what is called the "karate chop" spot on the outside of your hand (either one) between the bottom of your little finger and your wrist. (See the picture of where to tap.)

While tapping the karate chop spot with your pointer and middle fingers, say three times: "Even though I'm restless right now and can't think about my work, I'm really a good kid." (Or, "I'm okay," or "I like myself.") This part is called the kickoff.

Now tackle the tapping.

Go through the tapping spots on your body (see the picture), tapping about seven times on each of the eight spots and saying a "focus phrase" to keep you focused on the problem. In this example, the focus phrase can be "this restless feeling."

Start with your eyebrow and go down your body, ending up with your crown (top of the head). To do the tapping, use your pointer finger and middle finger together and the hand you normally use (just because it's easier—it really doesn't matter). You can tap on either side of the body (or both, if you want to give it extra oomph).

Rate the problem again.

When you have tapped one round, stop, tune in to the problem, and rate it again from 0 (gone) to 10 (horrible). Has it gone down? (Are you feeling less restless?) What is the number now?

If necessary, repeat the tapping.

If the problem is not at 0, repeat the tapping steps using the following words:

Kickoff: "Even though I still have some restlessness [or whatever the problem is], I'm a good kid." (Or, "Even though I'm still restless …")

Tapping Series Focus phrase: "Remaining [problem]" ("Remaining restlessness")

If something else comes up . . .

If something new about the situation comes up when you're tapping, you can tap on that, too. For example, maybe you realize that you're restless because you can't stop thinking about a particular thing. When you do the kickoff, say, "Even though I'm restless because I can't stop thinking about _____(whatever it is), I'm a good kid." Your focus phrase can be "thinking about _____" or just "_____." Maybe you have a hockey game later and you keep thinking about it. You can just say "hockey game" as your focus phrase. (You will probably play better when you get there!)

See if you can get to 0, and have fun!

Spots to Tap in the Tapping Game

Use these two fingers (either hand) to tap.

★ 8

1
★

★ 2

★ 3

4
★

★ 5

★ 6

★ 7

Karate Chop Spot

Tap the Karate Chop Spot on the side of either hand while you are saying the Kickoff. Tap spots 1-8 while you are saying the Focus Phrase. You may tap on <u>either side</u> of the body and use <u>either hand</u> to tap.

1 - On the inside of the eyebrow
2 - On the side of the eye
3 - Under the eye on the eye socket bone
4 - Under the nose
5 - Under the bottom lip

Spots to Tap in the Tapping Game

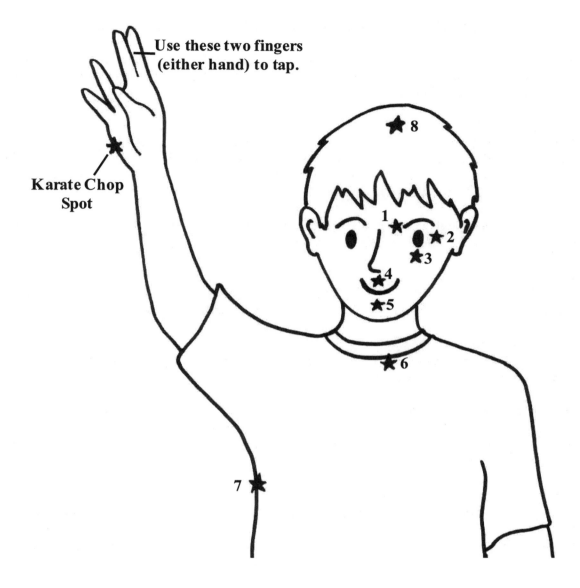

Use these two fingers (either hand) to tap.

Karate Chop Spot

Tap the Karate Chop Spot on the side of either hand while you are saying the Kickoff. Tap spots 1-8 while you are saying the Focus Phrase. You may tap on <u>either side</u> of the body and use <u>either hand</u> to tap.

1 - On the inside of the eyebrow
2 - On the side of the eye
3 - Under the eye on the eye socket bone
4 - Under the nose
5 - Under the bottom lip

6 - Just below the end of the collarbone
7 - Below the armpit 4 inches
8 - On the crown of the head
   (You can use all four fingers in a row
   along the top of the head.)

Uses for the Tapping Game

SAMPLE KICKOFFS AND FOCUS PHRASES FOR DIFFERENT SITUATIONS

Remember that the kickoff is said while you are tapping on the karate chop spot, and the focus phrase is said as you go through the rest of the tapping spots, tapping about seven times on each with your pointer and middle fingers.

IMPROVE PERFORMANCE:
Kickoff: "Even though I feel bad because I can't throw the ball very well, I'm a good kid and I like myself." *Focus phrase:* "Can't throw." (Don't worry if you don't really feel as if you like yourself. Just say it anyway. Or tap on: "Even though I don't really like myself because I can't throw very well, I'm okay and I'm a good kid.")

Kickoff: "Even though when I'm playing the flute, I always mess up on the hard parts, I'm okay and I accept myself." *Focus phrase:* "Mess up"

IMPROVE TEST SCORES:
Kickoff: "Even though I don't want to take this test because I'm afraid I'll flunk and it's making me nervous, I like myself and I'm really okay." *Focus phrase:* "This test"

HELP RELIEVE SADNESS:
Kickoff: "Even though my hamster died and I'm really sad, I like myself and I'm okay." *Focus phrase:* "My hamster" or "Very sad"

HELP RELIEVE ANGER:
Kickoff: "Even though I feel like knocking that guy out and I can't stand him, I'm a good kid." *Focus phrase:* "_____ (that guy's name)" or "Really mad!" (When you're tapping, say how you *really feel* about the situation. That and the tapping help release the feeling.)

SOMETIMES HELP RELIEVE PAIN:
Kickoff: "Even though my tummy hurts, I really like myself." *Focus phrase:* "Tummy hurts" (If you know why your tummy hurts, you can tap on that: "Even though my tummy hurts because I'm scared about _____, I like myself and I'm a good kid." *Focus phrase:* "Scared about ___"

GET OVER NIGHTMARES:
Kickoff: "Even though I'm having these icky nightmares and they're scaring me, I like myself and I'm okay." *Focus phrase:* "These nightmares." (Or get specific if you can: "Even though I woke up because a tiger was chasing me in my nightmare, I'm a good kid and *not* very tasty to tigers!" *Focus phrase:* "That terrible tiger!")

TRY IT ON EVERYTHING!
Whenever you have a feeling you're having trouble dealing with or that's really bothering you and keeping you from learning or getting along with others or enjoying life, try the Tapping Game on it. You may be surprised that it's no longer a problem.

Appendix Activity 17

Making Emotional Connections

A.   Choose one color of marker and write your name in the middle of the center circle.

B.   Now, with the same color in the same circle, write the names of the people you love who are closest to you, such as your mom, dad, sister/s, brother/s, grandparents, and other close family members.

C.   Next, choose another color, and in the second circle write the names of people you like and who are important to you but whom you aren't quite as close to as your family.

D.   Then, move on to the third circle and choose a third color. In this circle, write the names of people who play more minor roles in your life and whom you don't see as often but still care about and want to have in your life.

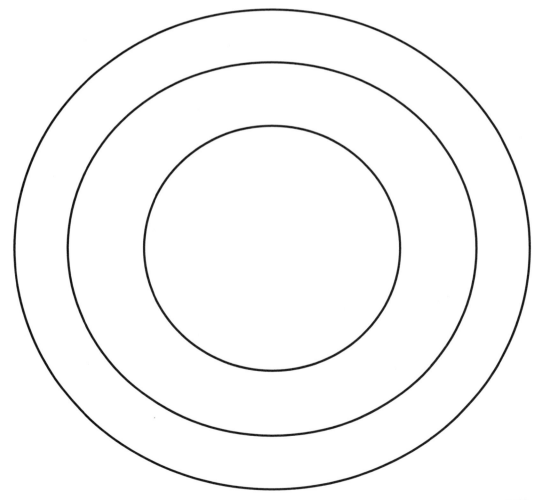

Making Emotional Connections, cont.

Complete the sentences using the same markers for the people as you did in the circles.

If I needed a hug, I would go to _____

_____

If I needed help to solve a problem, I would go to _____

_____

If I got scared, I would want to be with _____

_____

If I wanted to talk with someone, I would go to _____

_____

If I wanted to laugh and play, I would choose to be with _____

_____

If I wanted to tell someone something I did that I was proud of, I would go to _____

_____

If I was angry and wanted to "blow off steam," I would go to _____

_____

If I needed advice about how to make friends, I would go to _____

_____

If I felt I was treated unfairly by an adult, I would feel comfortable going to _____

_____

If I did something bad, I would be able to tell _____ about it.

If I wanted to go hiking to enjoy all the fun and beautiful things of nature, I would ask ____

_____ (may be more than one person) to go with me.

Appendix Activity 18
Labyrinth Adventure

Start here.

Appendix Activity 19

Guidelines for Creating a Friendship Space

The first two pages are for teachers or parents, depending on the venue. The third page is an example of a list of guidelines that could be posted in the Friendship Space for the children. You might want to have the children create and decorate their own poster, first brainstorming the guidelines with your help. That way, they have some ownership in the guidelines.

Space

Create a space that has room for up to six children at one time for talking and a bit of movement.

It is best to locate this space away from the central focus area of a room.

If you also have a Quiet Space or Peace Place in the room, have the location of the Friendship Space on the opposite side of the room.

Add other ideas as you and the children decide what else to take into consideration in choosing a space:

_____

_____

_____

_____

Materials

- a small table, two chairs, and four soft cushions for children to sit on the floor

- a variety of quiet-type games, such as checkers, chess, Chinese checkers, dominoes, and board games suitable for your specific age group

- a variety of fiction, nonfiction, picture, and poetry books for two or more children to look at together or take turns reading to each other

- a variety of puzzles that two or more children can work on together

- other items as you and the children think of them, remembering that you can always add materials and remove materials periodically

Guidelines for Creating a Friendship Space, cont.

Behaviors Expected

- No more than six children should use the space at one time. (You can select a different number depending on the space you have available and your group.)

- In times of high demand for the use of this space, provide a sign-up sheet for the children.

- Specific times for the use of this space are during independent work time after the children and their friends have finished their work, during designated recreation times, before school, during choice times, and other times that are appropriate.

- Have the children use soft voices in this area so as not to disrupt the other activities that are going on in the room at the same time.

- Everyone who uses this space is responsible for putting materials away and leaving the area ready for others to use.

- Add other behaviors as needed.

Guidelines for the Friendship Space

P l e a s e

HAVE NO MORE THAN SIX AT A TIME IN THE FRIENDSHIP SPACE.

SIGN UP TO USE THIS SPACE IF IT IS BUSY.

MEET HERE WITH FRIENDS WHEN YOU HAVE FINISHED YOUR WORK, BEFORE CLASS STARTS, OR DURING OTHER TIMES SET FOR THE FRIENDSHIP SPACE.

USE SOFT VOICES TO RESPECT THE REST OF THE CLASS.

PUT MATERIALS AWAY, AND LEAVE THIS SPACE TIDY AND READY FOR OTHERS.

T h a n k   Y o u !

Appendix Activity 20

Guidelines for Creating a Quiet Space

Note: The first two pages are for teachers or parents, depending on the venue. The third page is an example of a list of guidelines that could be posted in the Quiet Space for the children. You might want to have the children create and decorate their own poster, first brainstorming the guidelines with your help. That way, they have some ownership in the guidelines.

Space

Choose a space that is away from any traffic pattern and away from the central focus of the room.

Choose a space that can accommodate four children sitting on cushions.

If possible, create this space next to a natural lighting source.

Add other ideas that you and the children come up with to make this a special space for them to come to for quiet time:

_____

_____

_____

_____

Materials

- four soft, comfortable cushions on which the children using the area may sit

- a variety of books, individual brain-teaser puzzles, colored pencils, and drawing paper

- a variety of music selections that are quiet, welcoming, inspirational, and/or offer rich imagery backgrounds. (See suggestions given in *The Mozart Effect for Children* by Don Campbell and *Learn with the Classics* by Ole Anderson, Dr. Arthur Harvey, and Marcy Marsh, listed in the Resource section of this book.)

- four headsets and tape or DVD players

- other materials as appropriate for the age group using them

Behaviors Expected

Provide a sign-up sheet in case the space is busy.

Specific times for the use of this space are during independent work time after a child has finished his or her work, before school, during choice times, and other times that are appropriate, or designated or permitted by you.

Each child who uses this space is to honor the other children here by not sitting too close to them or talking to them.

Everyone who uses this space is responsible for putting away the materials they used and leaving the area ready for others.

Add other behaviors as needed.

<u>Guidelines for the Quiet Space</u>

P l e a s e

HAVE NO MORE THAN FOUR AT A TIME IN THE QUIET SPACE.

SIGN UP TO USE THIS SPACE IF IT IS BUSY.

ENJOY THIS SPACE WHEN YOU HAVE FINISHED YOUR WORK, BEFORE CLASS STARTS, DURING OTHER TIMES SET FOR THE QUIET SPACE, OR WITH PERMISSION.

ENJOY THIS SPACE WITHOUT TALKING.

ALLOW OTHERS TO HAVE THEIR OWN SPACE AROUND THEM.

PUT MATERIALS AWAY, AND LEAVE EVERYTHING TIDY AND READY FOR OTHERS TO USE.

T h a n k   Y o u !

What I Learned About the Natural Elements of Planet Earth

Three important things I learned are:

_____

_____

_____

Ideas I want to remember about:

earth (soil)	air
water	fire (light/heat/energy)

Other things I would like to know about one or more of the four elements are:

_____

_____

_____

_____

_____

Resources

Books for Teachers and Parents

Adams, Hetty. *Peace in the Classroom: Practical Lessons in Living for Elementary-Age Children.* Winnipeg, Manitoba: Portage & Main Publishing, 1994.

Anderson, Ole, Dr. Arthur Harvey, and Marcy Marsh. *Learn with the Classics: Using Music to Study Smart at Any Age (How to Use Music for Learning, Teaching, and Studying),* book and CD. San Francisco, California: LIND Institute, 1999. www.relaxwiththeclassics.com

Batmanghelidj, F., M.D. *Your Body's Many Cries for Water.* Falls Church, Virginia: Global Health Solutions, 1997.

Burns, Litany. *The Sixth Sense of Children: Nurturing Your Child's Intuitive Abilities.* New York: New American Library, a Division of Penguin Putnam Inc., 2002.

Campbell, Don G. *The Mozart Effect for Children: Awakening Your Child's Mind, Health, and Creativity with Music.* New York: HarperCollins Publishers, Inc., 2000.

Caduto, Michael J., and Joseph Bruchac. *Keepers of the Earth: Native American Stories and Environmental Activities for Children.* Golden, Colorado: Fulcrum Publishing, 1997.

Childre, Doc Lew. *Teaching Children to Love: 80 Games & Fun Activities for Raising Balanced Children in Unbalanced Times.* Boulder Creek, California: Planetary Publications, 1996.

Coles, Robert. *The Spiritual Life of Children.* Boston: Houghton Mifflin Company, 1990.

Drew, Naomi. *Learning the Skills of Peacemaking: A K-6 Activity Guide on Resolving Conflict, Communicating, and Cooperating.* Carson, California: Jalmar Press, 1995.

Emoto, Masaru. *Messages from Water.* Japan: I.H.M. General Research Institute, 1999.

Fredericks, Anthony. *Science Brainstretchers: Creative Problem-Solving Activities in Science.* Tucson, Arizona: Good Year Books, 1991.

Glazer, Steven, editor. *The Heart of Learning: Spirituality in Education.* New York: Penguin Putnam, 1999.

Hannaford, Carla, Ph.D. *Awakening the Child Heart: Handbook for Global Parenting.* Captain Cook, Hawaii: Jamilla Nur Publishing, 2002.

Henrikson, Peggy, and Lorraine O. Moore, Ph.D., with Linda LeClaire and Pamela S. Welter. *The Whole Kid Peace Activity Book: Promoting Self-Esteem, Preventing Conflict.* Available from Peytral Publications, Inc., Minnetonka, Minnesota, 1997.

Hubert, Bill. *Bal-A-Vis-X: Rhythmic Balance/Auditory/Vision eXercises for Brain and Brain-Body Integration.* Wichita, Kansas: Bal-A-Vis-X, Inc., 2001.

Iverson, Diane. *Discover the Seasons.* Nevada City, California: Dawn Publications, 1996.

Janke, Rebecca Ann, and Julie Penshorn Peterson. *Peacemaker's A,B,Cs: A Guide for Teaching Conflict Resolution with a Peace Table.* Marine on St. Croix, Minnesota: Growing Communities for Peace, 1995.

Janke, Rebecca Ann, and Julie Peterson. Peacemaker's Conflict Resolution Cubes. Marine on St. Croix, Minnesota: Growing Communities for Peace, 1995.

LIND Institute. *Relax with the Classics: Beautiful Music That's Good for You,* music series of 13 CDs. San Francisco, California: **LIND** Institute. www.relaxwiththeclassics.com

Moore, Lorraine O., Ph.D., and Peggy Henrikson. *Creating Balance in Children's Lives: A Natural Approach to Learning and Behavior.* Minnetonka, Minnesota: Peytral Publications, Inc., 2005.

Moore, Lorraine O., Ph.D. *Inclusion: Strategies for Working with Young Children—A Resource Guide for Teachers, Childcare Providers, and Parents.* Minnetonka, Minnesota: Peytral Publications, Inc., 2003.

Nabhan, Gary Paul, and Stephen Trimble. *The Geography of Childhood: Why Children Need Wild Places.* Boston, Massachusetts: Beacon Press, 1994.

Olson, Stuart Alve. *Tai Chi for Kids: Move with the Animals.* Rochester, Vermont: Bear Cub Books, 2001.

Roberts, Pamela. *Kids Taking Action: Community Service Learning Projects.* Northeast Foundation for Children, 2002.

Schmidt, Fran. *K-PAN: Kids Peace Action Network & the Peace Reporters.* Miami, Florida: Peace Education International, 1997.

Sears, William, M.D., and Martha Sears, R.N. *The Family Nutrition Book: Everything You Need to Know About Feeding Your Children—from Birth Through Adolescence.* Boston, Massachusetts: Little, Brown and Company, 1999.

Snow, Misti. *Take Time to Play Checkers: Wise Words from Kids on Their Parents, Friends, Worries, Hopes, and Growing Up.* New York: Viking Penguin, 1992.

Suzuki, David, and Amanda McConnell, with Maria DeCambra. *The Sacred Balance: A Visual Celebration of Our Place in Nature.* Vancouver, British Columbia: Greystone Books, A Division of Douglas & McIntyre Ltd., 2002.

Wolf, Aline. *Nurturing the Spirit in Non-Sectarian Classrooms.* Holidaysburg, Pennsylvania: Parent Child Press, 1996.

Books for Children

Bruchac, Joseph. *Rachel Carlson: Preserving a Sense of Wonder.* Golden, Colorado: Fulcrum Publishing, 2004.

Cain, Janan. *The Way I Feel.* Seattle, Washington: Parenting Press, 2000.

De Saint-Exupéry, Antoine. *The Little Prince.* New York: Harcourt, Brace & World, 1943.

Lewis, Barbara A. *A Kids Guide to Service Projects.* Minneapolis, Minnesota: Free Spirit Publishing, 1995.

Locker, Thomas. *John Muir: America's Naturalist.* Nevada City, California: Dawn Publications, 2004.

Locker, Thomas. *Walking with Henry: Based on the Life and Works of Henry David Thoreau.* Golden, Colorado: Fulcrum Publishing, 2002.

Payne, Lauren Murphy. *Just Because I Am.* Minneapolis, Minnesota: Free Spirit Publishing, 1994.

Reed-Jones, Carol. *The Tree in the Ancient Forest.* Nevada City, California: Dawn Publications, 1995.

Rink, Cindy. *Where Does the Wind Blow?* Nevada City, California: Dawn Publications, 1995.

Romain, Trevor, and Elizabeth Verdick. *Stress Can Really Get on Your Nerves!* Minneapolis, Minnesota: Free Spirit Publishing, 2000.

Suzuki, David, and Kathy Vanderlinden. *ECO-FUN: Great Projects, Experiments, and Games for a Greener Earth.* Vancouver/Toronto/New York: Greystone Books, Douglas & McIntyre Publishing Group, 2001.

Suzuki, David, and Kathy Vanderlinden. *You Are the Earth: Know the Planet So You Can Make It Better.* Vancouver/Toronto/New York: Greystone Books, Douglas & McIntyre Publishing Group, 1999.

Peytral Publications, Inc. is here to help you. If you have questions, comments, would like to place an order, or request a catalog, please contact us by mail, telephone, fax, or online. We will be happy to assist you!

Peytral Publications, Inc.
PO Box 1162
Minnetonka, MN 55345

To place an order call toll free: 1-877-PEYTRAL
All other questions or inquiries
Telephone (612) 949-8707
FAX (612) 906-9777
E-mail HELP@pevtral. com

For the most current listing of new titles and perennial best sellers, we encourage you to visit our web site at:

www.peytral.com